KILLING ME SOUFFLÉ

RATTLE·AND·YUM

/// OK·COMPOTE ///

APPETITE FOR DEGUSTATION

DARK SIDE OF THE SPOON

90 ROCKING RECIPES
THE TASTIEST ACTS IN ROCK 'N' ROLL, POP AND HIP HOP

WITH RECIPES COMPOSED BY KARINA DUNCAN

KYLE BOOKS

First published in Great Britain in 2015 by
Kyle Books, an imprint of Kyle Cathie Ltd
192–198 Vauxhall Bridge Road
London SW1V 1DX
general.enquiries@kylebooks.com
www.kylebooks.com

10 9 8 7 6 5 4 3 2 1

ISBN 978 0 85783 283 2

Project Editor: Tara O'Sullivan
Copy Editor: Stephanie Evans
Designer: Louise Leffler
Illustrator: Marylou Faure
Production: Nic Jones and Gemma John

A Cataloguing in Publication record for this title is available from the British Library.

Colour reproduction by ALTA London
Printed and bound in Malaysia by Tien Wah Press

FOR THOSE ABOUT TO WOK WE SALUTE YOU

ROCK 'N' ROLL

10

INTRODUCTION

8

EVERY GREAT DISH DESERVES A SOUNDTRACK

Like your dinner with a side of Madonna? Your cuisine with a pinch of Queen? Then get ready to experience the ultimate nosh pit.

Killing Me Soufflé is an epic kitchen gig celebrating the coming together of two of life's grooviest ingredients, music and food.

The greatest ever acts in Rock 'n' Roll, Pop, Hip Hop and RnB inspire 90 delectable duets that'll have you dishing up a string of chart toppers. Enjoy Crowd Warmers (starters), Headliners (main courses) and Encores (desserts) at each of the three stages.

It's like music to your mouth.

Bon Jovi Appétit!

ESSENTIAL INSTRUMENTS

ROCK 'N' ROLL
STAGE

LINE UP

RAGE AGAINST THE TAGINE
MOTLEY STEW
FLAN HALEN
STONE TEMPLE PINE NUTS
BLINK 18CHEW
FOOD FIGHTERS
MUNCHBOX TWENTY
ARCADE FRYER
SALMON & GARFUNKEL
NO TROUT
THE SEX PESTOS
HARISSA ETHERIDGE
FLEETWOOD MACARONI
ZZ CHOP
QUINCE OF THE STONE AGE
BUNS N' ROSES
HOOTIE & THE CRAYFISH

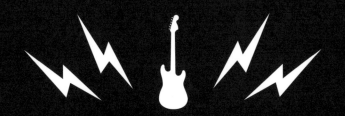

GRAIN DAY
SOY DIVISION
THE WHEAT STRIPES
CREDENCE BOIL WATER REVIVAL
NINE INCH SNAILS
ARCTIC MUNCHEES
CHEF LEPPARD
BREAD ZEPPELIN
JOHN NOUGAT MELLENCAMP
THE PEACH BOYS
LINKIN PORK
MOUSSE SPRINGSTEEN
THE ROLLING STOVES
CORDON BLUR

AND MORE...

CROWD WARMERS

SUMMER OF '60 NAAN

INDIAN SPICED AVOCADO DIP
WITH HOMEMADE NAAN BREAD

A REMIX OF: 'SUMMER OF '69' BY BRYAN ADAMS, 1985

Few opening riffs can lure a room of denim-clad air-guitar novices into communal song as well as this sentimental beauty from Canadian hit-machine Bryan Adams. And what do those same partygoers need? Snacks. Yummy snacks. So dish this one up, play it loud and sing: 'Those were the best dips of my life.'

Rock 'n' Roll

AVOCADO DIP:

2 teaspoons cumin seeds

3 ripe avocados, halved, pitted, peeled
    and diced

1 red chilli, finely chopped

3 tablespoons finely chopped coriander

1 spring onion, thinly sliced

2 tablespoons natural yogurt

zest and juice of 1 lime

salt and freshly ground pepper

NAAN BREAD:

450g strong plain flour, plus extra for dusting

7g sachet fast-action dried yeast

1 teaspoon salt

1 teaspoon caster sugar

7 tablespoons natural yogurt

2 tablespoons vegetable oil

vegetable oil spray, for baking

First make the naan dough. Use an electric mixer with a dough hook attachment to mix the flour, yeast, salt and sugar until combined (or mix by hand in a large mixing bowl). Pour in 185ml warm water, along with the yogurt and oil, and mix until the dough comes together. Continue mixing on a low speed for 4–5 minutes (alternatively, remove the dough from the bowl and knead by hand on a clean surface for 5 minutes or until smooth). Place the dough in a lightly floured bowl, cover with clingfilm and place in a warm place to rise for 1 hour or until the dough has doubled in size.

To make the avocado dip, toast the cumin seeds in a small frying pan over a medium heat for 2–3 minutes. Grind the seeds with a pestle and mortar until they form a powder. Transfer to a medium-sized bowl and combine with the avocados, chilli, coriander and spring onion. Use a fork to mix the ingredients together while coarsely mashing up the avocados. Add the yogurt, lime zest and juice, and a generous seasoning of salt and pepper. Mix to combine, then cover and refrigerate until the naan bread is ready.

Preheat the oven to 240°C/gas mark 9 and heat a pizza stone or a large baking tray for 25 minutes. Remove the dough from the bowl, place on a clean, lightly floured surface and knock back. Divide into six equal portions and roll each one into an oval shape about 15–20cm long. Spray each side of the dough with oil and place two or three pieces (depending on size) on the preheated stone or tray. Bake for 5–8 minutes or until puffed and slightly golden. Remove from the oven and wrap in foil to keep warm. Repeat with the remaining dough.

Serve the warm naan bread on a platter alongside the avocado dip.

Rock 'n' Roll

EVERY BROTH YOU TAKE

CHICKEN, GINGER & SWEETCORN SOUP

A REMIX OF: 'EVERY BREATH YOU TAKE' BY THE POLICE, 1983

The Police inspired our spin on this Chinese classic and this one's definitely worth a night in the clink. Our rendition introduces fresh coriander and ginger for some added Sting.

Rock 'n' Roll

900ml chicken stock

1 boneless, skinless chicken breast

1 teaspoon finely chopped fresh ginger

1 garlic clove, finely chopped

50g dry rice noodles

70g fresh sweetcorn kernels

2 spring onions, finely sliced

3 teaspoons dark soy sauce

2 tablespoons freshly chopped coriander

Pour the chicken stock into a large saucepan over a medium–high heat and add the chicken breast, ginger and garlic. Bring to the boil, then reduce the heat to low and simmer for 15 minutes or until the chicken has cooked through.

Remove the chicken from the pan and shred with a fork into bite-sized pieces.

Add the noodles, sweetcorn, half the spring onions and the soy sauce to the pan. Gently simmer for 4–5 minutes or until the noodles and sweetcorn are cooked, before returning the shredded chicken to the pan.

Serve the soup immediately with a sprinkling of the remaining spring onions and the coriander leaves.

• • • • • • • • • • •

'I FOUGHT THE SLAW AND THE SLAW WON'

Rock 'n' Roll

UNDER
THE FRIDGE

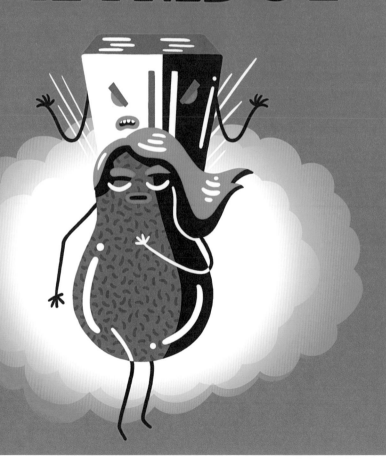

CEVICHE TOAST WITH AVOCADO & CORIANDER

A REMIX OF: 'UNDER THE BRIDGE' BY RED HOT CHILI PEPPERS, 1991

Inspired by this seminal rock tune by the Red Hot Chili Peppers, paradoxically this tangy delight is not red hot, nor does it contain chillies. To get started, hit the local markets for some really fresh fish or throw a line in 'under the bridge'. Any white fish will work with this recipe.

Serves: 8 as a canapé, 4 as a small starter
Preparation time: 10 minutes   Cooking time: 10 minutes

400g white fish (such as lemon sole, halibut or snapper), skinned and sliced into 1cm cubes
juice of 1 lime
2 shallots, thinly sliced
20g coriander leaves, chopped

1 avocado, halved, pitted, peeled and diced
8 slices sourdough baguette
2 tablespoons extra virgin olive oil
1 garlic clove, halved
salt and freshly ground black pepper

Put the cubed fish in a medium-sized bowl and combine with the lime juice, shallots, coriander and avocado. Season with salt and pepper to taste, and place in the fridge while preparing the toast.

Preheat a griddle pan over a high heat. Lightly brush the bread with the olive oil and place on the griddle for 1–2 minutes. Once the bread turns golden and begins to char, flip it over and grill for a further 1-2 minutes. Finish by rubbing the cut side of the garlic gently across the toast to infuse with its flavour.

Remove the ceviche from the fridge and spoon evenly over the pieces of toast. Serve immediately.

• • • • • • • • • • •

'I HAVE ONLY ONE BURNING DESIRE – LET ME STAND NEXT TO YOUR FRYER'

Rock 'n' Roll

POLENTA SANDMAN

THYME POLENTA CHIPS

A REMIX OF: 'ENTER SANDMAN' BY METALLICA, 1991

Metallica's dark, thunderous classic, with perhaps the most explosive of all rock intros, inspires these heavy-metal snacks. After all, you'll need some sustenance as a reward for the stovetop solos you'll be ripping out. Invite around all the local bikers, dress entirely in black and don't hold back on the volume.

Serves: 4   Preparation time: 10 minutes   Cooking time: 30 minutes (plus setting time)

olive oil, for greasing
1 litre vegetable or chicken stock
250g instant polenta
40g Parmesan, finely grated

vegetable oil, for deep-frying
1 tablespoon roughly chopped thyme leaves
salt and freshly ground black pepper

Lightly grease a 22 x 30cm baking tray with a little olive oil and set aside.

In a heavy-based saucepan, bring the stock to a boil over a medium-high heat. Gradually add the polenta in a steady stream, stirring with a whisk all the while, and continue to stir to combine. Reduce the heat to medium and, using a wooden spoon, stir for 2–3 minutes until the mixture thickens and softens. Remove from the heat and add the Parmesan.

Transfer the polenta to the greased tray and use the back of a spoon to spread it out evenly. Cover with a piece of baking paper and refrigerate for 3 hours or overnight.

Once set, turn out the polenta onto a board and slice into 2cm strips. Cut each strip into 8cm long chips. Heat the vegetable oil in a deep-fat fryer or heavy-based saucepan to 180°C. Fry the polenta chips, in batches, for 5 minutes or until golden brown. Drain on kitchen paper and keep warm while frying the remainder. Transfer the chips to a serving platter, sprinkle with thyme and season generously with salt and freshly ground pepper.

DON'T STOP THINKING ABOUT TOMATO

SAGANAKI WITH TOMATO, OLIVE & OREGANO SALAD

A REMIX OF: 'DON'T STOP' BY FLEETWOOD MAC, 1977

This incredible song is from Fleetwood Mac's 1977 hit album *Rumours*. Funny that, because there's also been plenty of gossip about the tomato... is it a fruit or a veggie? All we know is that the band achieved their complex sound by having three lead singers, so we've given our Greek salad three lead ingredients to complement the sharp and salty hot cheese.

Serves: 4   Preparation time: 10 minutes   Cooking time: 10 minutes

350g cherry tomatoes, halved
12 Kalamata olives, pitted and halved
½ red onion, thinly sliced
2 tablespoons oregano leaves
2 teaspoons red wine vinegar

3 tablespoons olive oil
500g halloumi or kefalograviera cheese,
  cut into thick slices
1 lemon, cut into wedges, to serve

Put the tomatoes in a medium-sized bowl with the olives, red onion, oregano, vinegar and 2 tablespoons of the olive oil. Toss gently until combined. Set aside.

Heat the remaining tablespoon of oil in a non-stick frying pan over a medium-high heat. Add the cheese and fry for 1–2 minutes until golden brown. Turn the cheese over and cook for a further 2 minutes or until golden.

Serve the hot cheese immediately with the salad and lemon wedges.

PRAWN RICE PAPER ROLLS WITH SWEET CHILLI DIPPING SAUCE

A REMIX OF: 'SWEET CHILD O' MINE' BY GUNS N' ROSES, 1988

Inspired by the monster track from the best-selling debut album ever in the USA comes our Appetiser for Destruction. The killer riff started out as one of Slash's warm-up exercises in jam sessions. Our succulent Vietnamese treats also act as a warm up, this time for the main course. They'll take you straight to Paradise City.

Serves: 4   Preparation time: 15 minutes   Cooking time: 15 minutes

RICE PAPER ROLLS:

100g rice vermicelli noodles
8 large round rice paper wrappers
8 cooked prawns, peeled, deveined and
    halved lengthways
3 tablespoons Thai basil leaves, left whole
3 tablespoons whole coriander leaves
1 cucumber, sliced into thin matchsticks
salt and freshly ground black pepper

DIPPING SAUCE:

4 tablespoons sweet chilli sauce
1 tablespoon lime juice
1 tablespoon fish sauce
1 tablespoon freshly chopped coriander
1 teaspoon sesame oil

To make the dipping sauce, put all the ingredients into a jar or small bowl, and mix well to combine. Set aside.

Cook the vermicelli noodles according to the packet instructions. Drain and set aside until cool.

To assemble the rolls, fill a large, flat dish with boiling water and dip one rice paper wrapper into it briefly to soften. Shake off any excess water, place the wrapper on a plate, and arrange two halves of a prawn, pink side down, in the middle of the wrapper. Top with a small bundle of noodles, a few basil and coriander leaves and a few sticks of cucumber. Season to taste, then roll up the rice paper (in the same way as a burrito), tucking in the sides as you go. Repeat to make eight rice paper rolls.

Once all the rolls have been made, serve immediately alongside the dipping sauce.

Rock 'n' Roll

SWEET
CHILLI
O'MINE

SPINACH & FETA FILO CIGARS

A REMIX OF: 'ANOTHER BRICK IN THE WALL' BY PINK FLOYD, 1979

These lovely vegetarian bites are inspired by one of the most influential and groundbreaking tracks in the history of rock 'n' roll, a three-part rock opera, part two of which was the only No. 1 single for Pink Floyd in the UK and USA. Summon a boys' choir to the kitchen and get cooking.

Rock 'n' Roll

Makes: around 20   Preparation time: 50 minutes   Cooking time: 25 minutes

700g baby leaf spinach
2 shallots, finely chopped
3 garlic cloves, finely chopped
400g feta cheese, crumbled
3 teaspoons ground sumac

zest of 1 lemon, plus 2 tablespoons juice
10 sheets filo pastry
150g unsalted butter, melted
salt and freshly ground black pepper

Preheat the oven to 180°C/gas mark 4.

Bring a large pot of water to the boil. Working in batches, blanch the spinach leaves for 30 seconds and use a slotted spoon to transfer to a colander. Repeat until all the spinach is blanched. Run the spinach under cold water until cool. Drain as much liquid as possible from the colander and then use your hands to squeeze any more excess liquid from the spinach.

Once the spinach is quite dry, coarsely chop and place in a large bowl. Add the shallots, garlic, feta and sumac and mix well with a fork. Season generously to taste with salt and pepper, add the lemon zest and juice, and stir to combine.

Place a sheet of filo pastry on a clean, dry surface (keep the remaining sheets covered with a damp cloth to prevent them from drying out). Brush the sheet of filo with melted butter and then place another sheet of filo on top to make two layers. Cut the filo into four equal strips and place a heaped tablespoon of filling at the end of each piece of filo. Carefully fold the edges in and roll tightly like a cigar. Repeat with the remaining sheets of filo and filling, and brush each with a little melted butter.

Place the filo cigars onto two lined baking trays. Bake for 20–25 minutes or until golden. Enjoy when nice and warm.

• • • • • • • • • • •

'WE ARE THE SULTANAS OF SWING'

BARBECUED SUMAC CALAMARI WITH LIME AIOLI

A REMIX OF: 'HOTEL CALIFORNIA' BY THE EAGLES, 1977

Inspired by the legendary rock tune about a life of excess in LA (something not unfamiliar to the Eagles), this lovely squid starter is far too special for any room service menu.

Serves: 4–6   Preparation time: 10 minutes   Cooking time: 15 minutes

CALAMARI:
800g calamari (squid) tubes, scored and
   cut into 2cm strips
2 tablespoons olive oil
2 teaspoons sumac
salt and freshly ground black pepper
juice of 1 lime, to serve

AIOLI:
4 egg yolks
2 teaspoons Dijon mustard
juice and zest of 1 lime
250ml light olive oil
4 garlic cloves, crushed

Mix together the calamari strips in a bowl with the olive oil and sumac and some salt and pepper. Refrigerate while making the aioli.

To make the aioli, put the egg yolks, mustard and lime juice in a food-processor. With the motor running, gradually add the oil. The mixture will turn into a mayonnaise and start to thicken. Add the garlic, lime zest and a pinch of salt and pepper.

Either place a large frying pan over a very high heat, or, if barbecuing, get a barbecue plate very hot, then add the calamari, tossing for 3–4 minutes or until it is just cooked through. Place in a bowl and squeeze over the lime juice. Serve alongside the aioli.

Rock 'n' Roll

YOU SHUCK ME ALL NIGHT LONG

OYSTERS WITH GREMOLATA SALT

A REMIX OF: 'YOU SHOOK ME ALL NIGHT LONG' BY AC/DC, 1980

If there's ever been an odd duet it's gotta be good old-fashioned rock 'n' roll and fancy pants oysters. Brian Johnson's first single behind the mic for AC/DC was an absolute pearler, and it inspires our swanky shellfish. Pop on your old school uniform and strut your stuff. Perhaps play some *Highway to Shell* with the leftovers?

Serves: 8   Preparation time: 5–10 minutes

3 tablespoons finely chopped flat-leaf parsley

½ tablespoon fine sea salt

1 garlic clove, finely crushed

2 teaspoons lemon zest

24 oysters, shucked and cleaned, in the half shell

1 tablespoon olive oil

freshly ground black pepper

Combine the parsley, salt, garlic and lemon zest in a small bowl. Ensure all ingredients are mixed well and season with pepper.

Sprinkle the gremolata salt over the oysters and drizzle over the olive oil.

Serve immediately.

BACON, GRUYÈRE & LEEK MUFFINS

A REMIX OF: 'MONEY FOR NOTHING' BY DIRE STRAITS, 1985

These country-kitchen savoury treats are influenced by the monster Dire Straits classic, with its amazing tension-building intro and one of the most brilliant-ever guitar riffs. Special cred goes to Sting for singing the backing vocals and the falsetto intro: 'I want my MTV'. Now it's your turn.

Makes: 12   Preparation time: 15 minutes   Cooking time: 30 minutes

butter, for greasing
1 tablespoon olive oil
3 back bacon rashers, finely chopped
½ leek, washed, dried and finely chopped
175ml milk

1 egg
120ml vegetable oil
150g Gruyère cheese, grated
2 tablespoons finely chopped chives
220g self-raising flour

Strap on your neon headband, roll up the sleeves on your blazer and preheat the oven to 180°C/gas mark 4. Grease a 12-hole muffin tin well with butter.

Heat the olive oil in a large frying pan over a medium heat. Add the bacon and leek, and stir for 5 minutes or until the leek softens and the bacon is golden. Drain and set aside to cool.

(Be careful: don't get a blister on your little finger, or a blister on your thumb.)

Lightly whisk the milk, egg and vegetable oil together in a medium-sized bowl. Add the cheese and chives, and the cooled leek and bacon. Stir to combine, but be careful not to overmix. Put the flour in a separate large bowl and make a well in the centre. Pour in the wet mixture and mix lightly. Spoon the mixture into the greased muffin tin until each hole is two-thirds full. Bake for 20–25 minutes or until browned on top. Remove the muffins from the tin and cool on a wire rack. Serve warm or at room temperature.

· · · · · · · · · · ·

'BUT SOME KIND OF MADRAS IS SWALLOWING ME WHOLE'

Rock 'n' Roll

'I WOULD DO ANYTHING FOR LOVE...

...BUT I WON'T CHEW THAT'

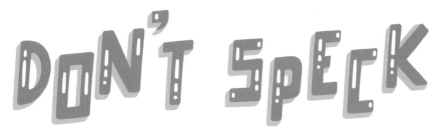

DON'T SPECK

SEARED SCALLOPS WRAPPED IN SPECK WITH HERB-SMASHED PEAS

A REMIX OF: 'DON'T SPEAK' BY NO DOUBT, 1996

Inspired by Gwen Stefani's song about her break-up from fellow No Doubt band member Tony Kanal, the only breaking up you'll be doing with these scallops is removing them from their shells. Aside from that, you'll want to be together forever. Enjoy. (Peroxide not required.)

Serves: 2   Preparation time: 10 minutes   Cooking time: 15 minutes

8 scallops, without roe
½ teaspoon ground coriander
1 lemon, zested then halved
2 tablespoons olive oil
8 thin slices of speck
2 shallots, sliced thinly

500g frozen peas
200ml chicken or vegetable stock
small handful each of mint and flat-leaf
   parsley, roughly chopped
salt and freshly ground black pepper

In a small bowl, toss together the scallops, coriander, lemon zest and half the olive oil. Wrap each scallop with a slice of speck, secure with a cocktail stick and refrigerate until required.

Add the remaining olive oil to a medium-sized saucepan and cook the shallots over a medium heat until softened slightly. Add the peas (gently so they aren't inflicted with black eyes) and the stock, and simmer for 5 minutes or until the peas are just tender. Remove from the heat, add the herbs and season with salt and pepper. Use a potato masher to coarsely mash the pea mixture. Cover to keep warm.

Preheat a large frying pan over a medium-high heat (or, if you are barbecuing, place a barbecue plate on a preheated barbecue). Fry the wrapped scallops for 2–3 minutes or until golden. Turn and fry for a further minute or until the scallops are medium-rare. Remove from the pan and serve with smashed peas and a good squeeze of lemon juice.

LADLE OF LOVE

BUTTERNUT SQUASH SOUP WITH HAZELNUT DUKKAH

A REMIX OF: 'CRADLE OF LOVE' BY BILLY IDOL, 1990

This metal-studded soup is a tribute to the UK wild boy of punk rock and his classic track about robbing the cradle. Inspired by Billy's reputation for being slightly bonkers, our nutty dukkah adds a wild zing to the finish. Lock up your daughters.

Rock 'n' Roll

BUTTERNUT SQUASH SOUP:

2 tablespoons olive oil

2 red onions, peeled and chopped

2 sticks of celery, chopped

2 carrots, peeled and chopped

3 garlic cloves, chopped

½ red chilli, deseeded and finely chopped

2kg butternut squash, deseeded and cut into medium-large dice

2 litres chicken or vegetable stock

salt and freshly ground black pepper

DUKKAH:

1 tablespoon fennel seeds

1 tablespoon cumin seeds

2 tablespoons coriander seeds

130g hazelnuts, roasted and skins removed

extra virgin olive oil, to serve

To make the soup, heat a large saucepan over a medium heat and add the olive oil. Add the onions, celery, carrots, garlic and chilli. Cook gently for 10 minutes or until the vegetables soften. Add the squash and stock to the pan and season with salt and pepper. Bring to the boil and simmer for 30 minutes.

To make the dukkah, toast the fennel, cumin and coriander seeds in a dry frying pan over a medium heat until the spices start to release a strong, toasty aroma and begin to colour slightly. Remove from the pan, cool for a few minutes and then combine with the hazelnuts in a food-processor. Pulse until finely chopped. Season with a little salt and pepper and set aside until needed.

Once the squash has cooked for 30 minutes and is soft, use a hand-mixer or blender to blend the soup until smooth. Check the seasoning and add more a little more salt and pepper if needed.

Divide the soup into bowls and sprinkle with a little dukkah and a drizzle of extra virgin olive oil.

Serve with a trademark Billy Idol attitude lip, sour squint and a raised, clenched fist in fingerless gloves.

Rock 'n' Roll

CORN FRITTERS WITH GUACAMOLE

A REMIX OF: 'BORN IN THE U.S.A' BY BRUCE SPRINGSTEEN, 1984

This tasty number will certainly establish you as *The Boss* of the kitchen. It's inspired by Bruce Springsteen's American cult hit, which deals with the hardships encountered by those returning home from the Vietnam War. Instead of wearing a hairnet, firmly tie your rolled-up bandana around your locks and get started.

Serves: 4   Preparation time: 15 minutes   Cooking time: 20 minutes

CORN FRITTERS:

420g fresh sweetcorn kernels

1 red onion, finely chopped

2 eggs

½ bunch coriander, roughly chopped

120g plain flour

1 teaspoon baking powder

1 small pinch of chilli flakes (optional)

4–5 tablespoons olive oil, for frying

GUACAMOLE:

3 ripe avocados, halved, pitted and peeled

2 shallots, finely chopped

1 red chilli, deseeded and finely chopped

½ bunch coriander, roughly chopped

zest and juice of 1 lime

10 cherry tomatoes, roughly chopped

salt and freshly ground pepper

To make the guacamole, put the avocado halves in a medium-sized bowl and roughly mash using the back of a fork, leaving some chunky bits. Add the shallots, chilli, coriander and lime zest and juice, and mix through with the fork. Season generously with salt and pepper and then fold through the chopped tomatoes. Cover and refrigerate until needed.

Place two thirds of the sweetcorn in a food-processor, along with the onion, eggs, coriander, flour, baking powder, chilli flakes (if desired) and a good pinch of salt and pepper, and pulse until combined. Transfer to a large bowl and stir through the remaining corn kernels.

In a large non-stick frying pan, heat some of the olive oil over a medium-high heat. Working in batches, drop heaped tablespoonfuls of the mixture into the pan and cook for 2–3 minutes on each side or until golden. Keep warm until all the fritters are cooked.

Serve with a heaped spoonful of guacamole over the warm fritters.

Rock 'n' Roll

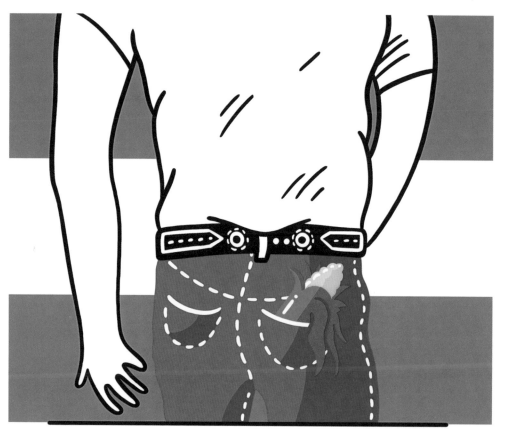

CORN IN THE USA

HEADLINERS

WHEN I CRUMB AROUND

WILD MUSHROOM RAGOÛT WITH CRUSTY GARLIC SOURDOUGH

A REMIX OF: 'WHEN I COME AROUND' BY GREEN DAY, 1995

This hearty winter-warmer is inspired by the massive fourth single from Green Day's game-changing album *Dookie* – green being the colour of food envy, of course. So spike your hair, apply a touch of guyliner and raise a middle finger to crap food.

Rock 'n' Roll

60ml olive oil

40g unsalted butter

300g mixed wild mushrooms, halved if large

2 shallots, finely chopped

3 garlic cloves, 2 finely chopped and
  1 halved

60ml dry white wine

4 slices of rustic sourdough bread

2 tablespoons freshly chopped flat-
  leaf parsley

1 tablespoon extra virgin olive oil

salt and freshly ground black pepper

Heat the oil and half the butter in a large frying pan over a medium-high heat. Cook the mushrooms for 1–2 minutes until they start to soften and wilt. Remove from the pan and set aside. Add the remaining butter to the frying pan, along with the shallots and chopped garlic. Stir over a medium heat until soft, then add the white wine and cook for a few minutes until the wine evaporates. Return the mushrooms to the pan and toss to combine. Cover to keep warm.

Meanwhile, toast the bread on a preheated griddle pan for 2–3 minutes on each side or until lightly charred. Rub one side of each slice with the cut sides of the halved garlic cloves.

Stir the parsley into the mushroom mixture and season well with salt and pepper. Serve a large spoonful of the mushroom ragoût on top of the toast and drizzle with a little extra virgin olive oil.

• • • • • • • • • • •

'THURSDAY I DON'T CARE ABOUT YOU IT'S FRIED EGGS I'M IN LOVE'

Rock 'n' Roll

CHINESE BARBECUED DUCK & SHIITAKE PASTRIES

A REMIX OF: 'SPACE ODDITY' BY DAVID BOWIE, 1969

Like the tune that inspired them, these delicious pastries are totally out of this world. If they had these in space, you'd never come down.

Serves: 8   Preparation time: 30 minutes   Cooking time: 40–45 minutes

50g dried shiitake mushrooms
1 tablespoon olive oil
1 onion, finely chopped
2 garlic cloves, finely chopped
2 teaspoons plain flour
1 teaspoon Chinese five-spice

1 Chinese barbecued duck (available from Asian barbecue or takeaway shops), meat removed and cut into bite-sized pieces
1 tablespoon dark soy sauce
4 sheets frozen puff pastry, thawed
1 egg, lightly beaten
freshly ground black pepper
hoisin sauce, to serve

Preheat the oven to 180°C/gas mark 4 and line two baking trays with baking paper.

Put the shiitake mushrooms in a bowl and cover with boiling water. Leave to soak for 10–15 minutes until softened. Drain the mushrooms, reserving 120ml of the soaking liquid.

Place a large frying pan over a medium heat. Add the oil and onion to the pan and stir for 3 minutes or until the onion softens. Add the garlic and continue to cook for another minute. Add the flour and Chinese five-spice, and cook for a minute more. Add the reserved shiitake soaking liquid and cook until the sauce begins to thicken, stirring constantly. Add the duck, soy sauce and a pinch of black pepper, and stir through to combine. Remove the pan from the heat and cool for 15 minutes.

Cut each sheet of pastry into four large squares. Place four squares on each baking tray and, leaving a finger-width edge around each square, divide the cooled filling between them. Use a pastry brush to brush the egg around the edge of each pastry square, before topping each with the remaining pastry squares. Use a fork to seal around the edge of each square, pressing the prongs down gently. Brush the tops of the squares with more egg and bake for 20–25 minutes or until puffed and golden.

Serve immediately with some hoisin sauce in a slow-mo, zero gravity kinda way.

HIT ME WITH YOUR BEST SHALLOT

MUSSELS WITH SHALLOTS & CREAMY WHITE WINE BROTH

A REMIX OF: 'HIT ME WITH YOUR BEST SHOT' BY PAT BENATAR, 1980

Pint-sized Pat Benatar broke onto the scene in the early 80s with her own brand of chick rock with muscle. So why not mussels with chick rock? This French culinary special punches well above its weight. So shell out on a copy of *Crimes of Passion*, get cooking and hit 'em in the mouth.

Serves: 4   Preparation time: 15 minutes   Cooking time: 10 minutes

1 tablespoon unsalted butter

2 large shallots, finely chopped

2 bay leaves

6 sprigs of thyme

1.8kg mussels, cleaned, beards removed
   (discard any mussels that are not closed)

100ml dry white wine

30ml single cream

4 tablespoons chopped flat-leaf parsley

salt and freshly ground black pepper

crusty bread, to serve

Select a pan that is large enough to hold all the mussels and which has a tight-fitting lid. Melt the butter in the pan over a medium-high heat. Once the butter has melted, add the shallots, bay leaves and thyme sprigs. Fry for 1–2 minutes.

Add the mussels and white wine and cover with the lid. Cook for 4–5 minutes or until the mussels have opened. Discard any that remain closed. Add the cream and chopped parsley and stir well. Season with salt and pepper to taste.

Serve immediately alongside crusty bread.

Rock 'n' Roll

THE FENNEL COUNTDOWN

BRAISED FENNEL WITH SMOKED SALMON ON SOURDOUGH

A REMIX OF: 'THE FINAL COUNTDOWN' BY EUROPE, 1986

If there was ever a keyboard riff to get you fist-pumping as you enter the kitchen, this is it. 'Sweden' was too feeble a title for this band. They went big, and so did their sound. And their hair. And now they need big flavour. Stopwatches at the ready. 3, 2, 1...

Serves: 4   Preparation time: 10 minutes   Cooking time: 40 minutes

3 tablespoons olive oil

3 garlic cloves, halved

2 large fennel bulbs, cut into 2cm wedges

400ml chicken stock

zest of 1 orange, pared off in 1 piece

4 thick slices of sourdough

8 slices of smoked salmon

salt and freshly ground black pepper

Put 2 tablespoons of the olive oil in a medium-sized saucepan over a medium heat and add the garlic. As the garlic turns golden-brown, remove with a slotted spoon and discard – the oil will be infused with its flavour. Add the fennel wedges to the pan and season with salt and pepper. Sauté the fennel for 2–3 minutes or until it begins to turn brown. Add the stock and the orange zest. Reduce the heat to a simmer and cook, covered, for 20–25 minutes or until the fennel is tender. Remove the fennel and set aside to cool slightly.

While the fennel cools, toast the bread. Drizzle the remaining olive oil over the slices of toast, and top each slice with the warm braised fennel. Gently lay over slices of smoked salmon and season generously with freshly ground pepper.

Serve immediately.

EYE OF THE TIKKA

CHICKEN TIKKA WITH MINTED COUSCOUS & YOGURT

A REMIX OF: 'EYE OF THE TIGER' BY SURVIVOR, 1982

Get fired up for this knockout dish with the best adrenalin-fuelled tune of all. We have Sly Stallone to thank for this recipe's soundtrack. After permission was rejected for the use of Queen's 'Another One Bites the Dust' in *Rocky III*, he requested the creation of this song from Survivor. Thanks, big guy.

Rock 'n' Roll

Serves: 4   Preparation time: 15 minutes   Cooking time: 20 minutes (plus marinating time)

CHICKEN TIKKA:

900g chicken mini fillets (or breast meat, thinly sliced)

½ teaspoon chilli powder

1 teaspoon turmeric

1 teaspoon ground cumin

3 teaspoons garam masala

1 tablespoon freshly grated ginger

200g natural yogurt, plus 4 tablespoons to serve

COUSCOUS:

375ml chicken stock

300g couscous

1 tablespoon butter

4 tablespoons roughly chopped mint leaves

1 lemon, cut into wedges

salt and freshly ground black pepper

Place all the chicken tikka ingredients in a medium-sized bowl. Stir to combine and coat the chicken well. Cover with clingfilm and place in the refrigerator to marinate for 1 hour.

Meanwhile, prepare the couscous. Pour the stock into a medium-sized saucepan and bring to the boil over a medium-high heat. When the stock comes to the boil, remove from the heat and add the couscous. Set aside, covered, for 4 minutes or until the stock is absorbed. Add the butter and mint, and season with salt and pepper. Use a fork to combine and fluff up the grains, then cover to keep warm.

Preheat a barbecue or place a griddle pan over a high heat. Grill the chicken in batches, cooking for 2–3 minutes on each side or until charred and cooked through.

Serve the chicken alongside the minted couscous and top with a spoonful of yogurt and a squeeze of lemon.

Rock 'n' Roll

LAMB MEATBALLS & TZATZIKI PITTA POCKETS

A REMIX OF: 'BITTER SWEET SYMPHONY' BY THE VERVE, 1997

Our composition of Turkish ingredients is inspired by The Verve's defining Britpop anthem. Interestingly, the famous strings section in this song is based on the Andrew Loog Oldham orchestral version of The Rolling Stones' 1965 song 'The Last Time'. These pitta pockets are so utterly delicious that finishing them will be bittersweet.

Serves: 4–6   Preparation time: 20 minutes   Cooking time: 15 minutes

MEATBALLS:

500g minced lamb

2 shallots, finely chopped

2 garlic cloves, crushed

1 tablespoon pine nuts, lightly toasted

1 teaspoon ground cumin

½ teaspoon ground coriander

½ teaspoon ground cinnamon

30g fresh breadcrumbs

2 tablespoons tomato purée

salt and freshly ground black pepper

2 tablespoons olive oil

TZATZIKI:

215g Greek-style yogurt

1 Lebanese cucumber, grated and squeezed of excess liquid (if you can't get hold of a Lebanese cucumber, an ordinary one will work just as well)

1 garlic clove, crushed

2 tablespoons roughly chopped mint

TO SERVE:

1 handful rocket

4 pitta breads, sliced in half

Put all the meatball ingredients except the olive oil into a large bowl, season with salt and pepper and mix well (the best way is to use your hands). Shape into roughly 24–28 small balls and place on a tray lined with baking paper. Refrigerate for 15–20 minutes.

To make the tzatziki, combine the yogurt, cucumber, garlic and mint in a medium-sized bowl and season with salt and pepper. Mix well and chill until needed.

To cook the meatballs, heat the oil in a frying pan over a medium-high heat. Working in two batches, cook the meatballs until golden brown on all sides and cooked through.

To serve, open a halved pitta pocket and tuck in some rocket leaves. Top with a few meatballs and a generous dollop of tzatziki.

PARMA POLICE

PROSCIUTTO-WRAPPED BEEF FILLET WITH POMEGRANATE & LEAFY GREENS

A REMIX OF: 'KARMA POLICE' BY RADIOHEAD, 1997

There are definitely no flavour police on duty for tonight's shift. Radiohead's iconic 'Karma Police' revolves around the premise of cause and effect. And if this topcut was dished up in return for doing something nice, the world would be a better place. You might not understand the lyrics but our rendition is a pretty simple guide to Pleasureville.

Rock 'n' Roll

7 slices of prosciutto (Parma ham)

700g fillet of beef

4 tablespoons Dijon mustard

4 tablespoons olive oil

50g baby leaf spinach

50g baby rocket

2 baby fennel, thinly sliced

seeds from ½ pomegranate

2 tablespoons lemon juice

salt and freshly ground black pepper

Start by preheating the oven to 200°C/gas mark 6.

Lay the slices of prosciutto in a row, side by side and slightly overlapping. Brush the fillet of beef with the mustard and lay across the prosciutto. Season generously with pepper, and gently roll up the prosciutto to enclose the beef. Place the wrapped beef, seam side down, on a roasting tray and drizzle with 2 tablespoons of olive oil. Roast for 30–35 minutes for medium, or cook until done to your liking (no longer than 40–45 minutes). Transfer the beef to a plate, and allow it to rest for 10 minutes.

Meanwhile, place the spinach, rocket, fennel and pomegranate seeds in a salad bowl. Drizzle with the remaining olive oil and the lemon juice. Season with salt and pepper and toss gently.

To serve, cut the fillet of beef into thick slices and serve alongside the salad.

• • • • • • • • • • •

'A SAFFRON NATION ARMY COULDN'T HOLD ME BACK'

Rock 'n' Roll

GIMME SHOULDER

CHARGRILLED MARINATED LAMB SHOULDER WITH MOZZARELLA & PEA SALAD

A REMIX OF: 'GIMME SHELTER' BY THE ROLLING STONES, 1969

The Rolling Stones are the most enduring act in music, infusing flavours of blues and rock into classic after classic. Like 'Born in the U.S.A.', this incredible song also describes the troubled era of the Vietnam War. But what do you serve to rock 'n' roll royalty? For the biggest lips in music it's gotta be a feast of burden. Now strut your stuff.

Rock 'n' Roll

4 garlic cloves, crushed

1 bunch oregano, leaves picked

1 tablespoon salt

4 tablespoons olive oil

zest of 1 and juice of ½ lemon, plus 1 to serve

1 lamb shoulder (around 1–1.5kg), boned,
    butterflied and trimmed of fat

300g fresh or frozen peas

375g fresh mozzarella

1 bunch of mint, leaves picked

100g pea shoots or baby rocket

salt and freshly ground black pepper

Use a pestle and mortar (or small food-processor) to pound together the garlic, oregano, salt, 2 tablespoons of the olive oil and the lemon zest. Place the lamb into a large glass or ceramic dish, and rub the mixture over the meat. Cover and place in the fridge to marinate. After 1 hour, remove the lamb from the fridge and allow 15 minutes for it to come to room temperature.

Preheat a barbecue or place a griddle pan over a high heat. Cook the lamb on the hot grill for 5–8 minutes on each side, then reduce the heat to low and continue cooking until the lamb is cooked to your liking (as a guide, a further 10–15 minutes will cook it medium). Transfer the lamb to a board or plate and cover with foil. Leave to rest for 10–15 minutes.

Meanwhile, bring a small pot of water to the boil and blanch the peas for 3–5 minutes or until tender. Drain and refresh under cold water. Drain again and place the peas in a medium-sized bowl. Tear the mozzarella into large pieces and add to the bowl along with the mint, pea shoots or baby rocket, remaining olive oil and the lemon juice. Season with salt and pepper and gently toss to combine.

Cut the lamb into thick slices and arrange on a serving platter alongside the pea and mozzarella salad.

Serve immediately with wedges of the remaining lemon.

Rock 'n' Roll

KNOCKIN' ON OVEN'S DOOR

MARINATED LAMB RACKS WITH HONEY-ROASTED BABY ROOT VEGETABLES

A REMIX OF: 'KNOCKIN' ON HEAVEN'S DOOR' BY BOB DYLAN, 1973

This here tasty roast is inspired by one of the biggest hits from the prolific folk-rock singer-songwriter Bob Dylan – a song covered by the likes of Eric Clapton and Guns N' Roses. The original tells the tale of a fading deputy sheriff, dying from a bullet wound. Our cover is the story of tender juicy lamb racks, beautifully seasoned and served with sweet crunchy veggies.

Rock 'n' Roll

2 lamb racks (4 cutlets per rack),
  French trimmed
2 teaspoons dried mint
4 garlic cloves, crushed
zest of 1 lemon
4 tablespoons olive oil

300g baby carrots, trimmed and washed
400g baby beetroots, trimmed, washed and
  halved
8 new or baby potatoes, halved
2 tablespoons runny honey
salt and freshly ground black pepper

Place the lamb racks in a bowl with the mint, garlic, lemon zest and 2 tablespoons of the olive oil. Toss to coat, then cover and refrigerate for at least 30 minutes.

Preheat the oven to 200°C/gas mark 6. Divide the vegetables and potatoes between two baking trays and drizzle with the remaining olive oil. Season with salt and pepper. Roast for 35 minutes.

Meanwhile, heat a large frying pan over a medium-high heat. Season the lamb racks and then cook, fat side down, turning occasionally, for 4–5 minutes or until golden brown. Transfer to an oven tray.

Now remove the vegetables from the oven and drizzle over the honey. Mix well so that they are evenly coated. Return the vegetables to the oven, along with the lamb racks. Roast for 8–10 minutes or until the vegetables are shiny, golden and cooked through and the lamb is medium–rare (or a little longer if you prefer your lamb well done). Be patient. Don't go knock knock knockin' on oven's door too early. Remove from the oven.

Keep the vegetables warm and let the lamb rest for 8–10 minutes before carving into cutlets and serving with the vegetables.

• • • • • • • • • • •

'THAT'S ME IN THE CORNER
LOSING MY REDUCTION'

BROWN SUGAR & LIME GLAZED SALMON WITH STICKY RICE

A REMIX OF: 'DAZED & CONFUSED' BY LED ZEPPELIN, 1969

Jimmy Page famously strums his guitar with a violin bow in this early Led Zeppelin belter. If there's a spare bow lying around the house, we suggest you do the same, practising on your frying pan as you warm up in the kitchen.

Serves: 4   Preparation time: 10 minutes
Cooking time: 20 minutes (plus rice cooking time)

2 tablespoons vegetable or coconut oil
1 red onion, thinly sliced
3 garlic cloves, finely chopped
3 tablespoons dark soy sauce
3 tablespoons fish sauce

100g brown sugar
juice of 1 lime, plus 1 lime, quartered, to serve
4 x 180g skinless salmon fillets
200g sushi rice or similar Japanese rice
freshly ground black pepper

Cook the rice according to the packet instructions.

Meanwhile, heat 1 tablespoon of the oil in a medium-sized saucepan over a medium heat. Add the onion and garlic and cook for a few minutes until softened. Stir in the soy sauce, fish sauce, sugar and the lime juice. Cook for a further 2–3 minutes until the sugar dissolves and the mixture becomes syrupy. Season with freshly ground black pepper, set aside and keep warm.

Heat the remaining oil in a large non-stick frying pan over a high heat. Cook the salmon fillets for 2–3 minutes on each side until is cooked, but still a little rare in the centre.

Serve the salmon on a platter or plate and pour over the syrupy glaze, covering each fillet generously. Serve alongside the hot sticky rice and lime wedges.

MEX ON FIRE

PULLED PORK TACOS

A REMIX OF: 'SEX ON FIRE' BY KINGS OF LEON, 2008

This spicy number is inspired by Nashville's best-groomed family and their arena rock ballad whose chorus sends women's hearts aflutter. No doubt they've pulled some chicks in their time – now it's time to pull some pork.

Rock 'n' Roll

Serves: 6–8   Preparation time: 10 minutes   Cooking time: 6 hours (including resting time)

2 tablespoons salt

2 tablespoons dark muscovado sugar

1 tablespoon smoked paprika

2kg pork shoulder, bone in

125ml apple juice

12 soft corn tortillas

hot pepper sauce and coleslaw, to serve

Preheat the oven to 200°C/gas mark 6. Mix together the salt, sugar and paprika in a small bowl.

Place the pork in a large roasting tin lined with foil. Sprinkle over half of the salt and sugar mixture and rub into the meat.

Cook the pork in the oven for 40 minutes or until browned. Pour over the apple juice and cover completely with foil. Reduce the heat to 120°C/gas mark ½ and cook slowly for a further 5½ hours or until the meat is very tender and falling off the bone.

Increase the heat to 220°C/gas mark 7. Uncover the pork and cook for a further 10 minutes so that the meat becomes crispy. Remove from the oven and leave to rest for 20 minutes.

Use forks or your fingers to shred the meat off the bone. Place in a bowl and pour over a few tablespoons of the pan juices. Stir through the remaining sugar and salt seasoning.

Heat the tortillas according to packet instructions and place a large spoonful of shredded pork in each tortilla. Top with coleslaw and serve with hot sauce.

• • • • • • • • • • •

'EVERY DAY SHOULD BE A HOLLANDAISE'

Rock 'n' Roll

PROSCIUTTO, MOZZARELLA & ROCKET PIZZA

A REMIX OF: 'ANOTHER ONE BITES THE DUST' BY QUEEN, 1980

If there's one thing to put on your bucket list before biting the dust, it's this Italian tastebud bonanza. It'll surely have you crowned Queen of la pizza. Press play on this royal ripper and let John Deacon's distinctive bassline set your tempo in the kitchen.

Serves: 2–3   Preparation time: 60 minutes   Cooking time: 20 minutes

BASE:
7g sachet fast-action dried yeast
a pinch of caster sugar
190g plain flour, plus extra for dusting
½ teaspoon salt
2 teaspoons olive oil, plus extra for greasing

TOPPING:
40ml extra virgin olive oil
1 teaspoon dried oregano
200g buffalo mozzarella, torn
50g firm mozzarella, grated
5 thin slices prosciutto
50g rocket
½ lemon
salt and freshly ground black pepper

Combine the yeast, sugar and 185ml warm water in a jug. Set aside in a warm place for 10–15 minutes until small bubbles start to appear on the surface.

Tip the flour and salt into a large bowl and make a well in the centre. Pour in the yeast mixture and use your hands to mix into a dough. Transfer to a lightly floured surface and knead for 4–5 minutes or until smooth and elastic. Place in a lightly oiled bowl, cover with clingfilm and rest in a warm place for 30 minutes or until doubled in size.

Preheat the oven to 250°C/gas mark 9. Lightly brush a large tray or pizza tray with the 2 teaspoons olive oil and dust with flour. On a lightly floured surface, roll out the dough to a circle measuring 40–50cm in diameter and transfer to the tray. For the topping, drizzle with olive oil, sprinkle with the oregano and top with the cheeses. Season and bake for 10–15 minutes or until the dough is golden and the cheeses have melted.

Lay the slices of prosciutto evenly over the pizza. Put the rocket in a small bowl, squeeze over the lemon juice and toss to combine. Top the pizza with the rocket and serve.

GRILLING IN THE NAME

GRILLED PEACHES WITH RICOTTA & SUGARED PISTACHIOS

A REMIX OF: 'KILLING IN THE NAME' BY RAGE AGAINST THE MACHINE, 1992

Hungry for a kitchen revolution? Protest against the ills of society with these luscious stone-fruit sensations, inspired by RATM's powerful anger-fuelled signature track – one of the greatest of the rap metal genre.

Rock 'n' Roll

Serves: 8   Preparation time: 15 minutes   Cooking time: 30 minutes

4 ripe peaches, pitted and halved

60g brown sugar

2 tablespoons unsalted butter

4 tablespoons ricotta cheese

PISTACHIOS:

2 tablespoons icing sugar

4 tablespoons pistachios

Do not direct any rage towards the oven, this is not 'the machine'. Just preheat it to 200°C/gas mark 6, and line a baking tray with baking paper.

To make the sugared pistachios, mix the icing sugar and pistachios in a small bowl with 2 teaspoons of water. Tip the pistachios onto the prepared tray, spread out in an even layer and bake for 8–10 minutes. Remove from the oven and allow to cool.

Meanwhile, place the peach halves, cut side up, in a single layer in a rectangular baking dish. Sprinkle over the brown sugar and divide the butter between the peaches. Bake for 10–12 minutes or until the sugar and butter melts and starts to bubble. Remove the peaches from the oven.

Preheat the grill to high. Divide the ricotta between the peaches. Once the grill is hot, grill the peaches for 5–6 minutes or until the ricotta starts to turn golden. Remove from the oven and serve the warm peaches on a plate with the sugared pistachios.

Make sure you don't lose any pistachios in the mosh pit.

• • • • • • • • • • •

'I'M A CRÊPE. I'M A WEIRDO'

Rock 'n' Roll

DUDE COOKS LIKE A LADY

PANCAKES WITH MIXED BERRY COMPOTE

A REMIX OF: 'DUDE (LOOKS LIKE A LADY)' BY AEROSMITH, 1987

Apparently based on Mötley Crüe's Vince Neil (as 'the dude' who looks like a lady), this great track became one of the biggest for the bad boys of Boston. Well guys, if the apron fits, wear it.

Serves: 4   Preparation time: 10 minutes   Cooking time: 15 minutes

PANCAKES:
125g self-raising flour
1 tablespoon caster sugar
a pinch of salt
75ml milk
1 egg
20g unsalted butter, melted, for brushing

MIXED BERRY COMPOTE:
45g caster sugar
300g fresh or frozen mixed berries
    (blueberries, raspberries, blackberries)
zest of ½ orange

To make the compote, put the sugar and 2 tablespoons of water in a small saucepan. Stir over a low heat until the sugar dissolves. Add the berries, increase the heat to high and boil for 3–5 minutes or until the berries begin to break down. Once the mixture thickens slightly, remove from the heat, stir through the orange zest and set aside.

For the pancake batter, mix the flour, sugar and salt together in a medium bowl. In a separate bowl, whisk together the milk and egg, then add to the dry ingredients. Whisk until smooth.

Heat a non-stick frying pan over a medium heat and brush with the butter. Drop tablespoonfuls of batter into the pan and cook for 1 minute or until small bubbles appear on the surface. Turn over and cook for a further minute or until golden. Remove from the pan to a plate and cover with a tea towel to keep warm. Continue to cook in batches, brushing the pan with more butter before each batch.

Serve the pancakes slightly warm or at room temperature, drizzled with the compote.

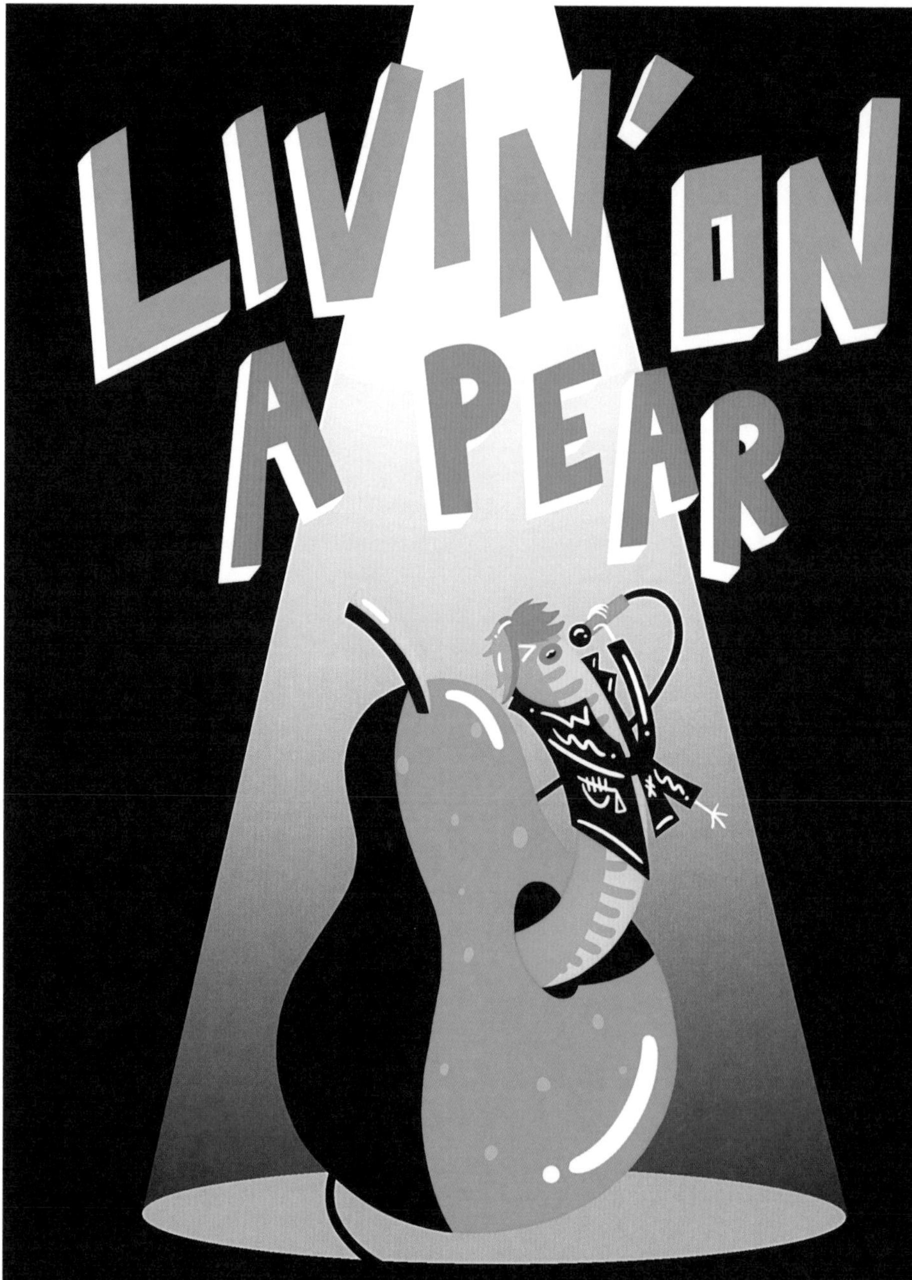
LIVIN' ON
A PEAR

HONEY, PEAR & GINGER CAKE
WITH VANILLA CREAM

A REMIX OF: 'LIVIN' ON A PRAYER' BY BON JOVI, 1986

This oven-baked stadium-lifter is inspired by every drunk man's karaoke go-to track and Bon Jovi's signature sound. The song is about a working-class couple who struggle to make ends meet. Obviously, we've taken some creative licence, as our glorious cake screams nothing but upper-class extravagance.

Serves: 16   Preparation time: 30 minutes   Cooking time: 90 minutes (including cooling time)

175g unsalted butter, at room temperature

250g dark brown sugar

2 pears (William or Bartlett), cores removed
    and each cut into 1cm-thick slices

390g plain flour

1 teaspoon bicarbonate of soda

2 tablespoons ground ginger

2 teaspoons mixed spice

140g treacle

140g runny honey

3 eggs

250ml buttermilk

VANILLA CREAM:

seeds from 1 vanilla pod

300ml whipping cream

35g icing sugar

Preheat the oven to 160°C/gas mark 3. Line a 22cm round cake tin with baking paper.

Melt 50g of the butter in a large frying pan over a medium heat. Once the butter starts to foam, scatter over half of the brown sugar and 1 tablespoon water, then continue to cook for a few minutes until the sugar dissolves completely.

Add the pears to the pan and stir to coat. Reduce the heat slightly and continue to cook for 8–10 minutes or until tender and the liquid thickens. Transfer the pears to the base of the cake tin in an even layer. Set aside.

Be careful, as the worktop may be 'slippery when wet'.

CONTINUED OVERLEAF

Rock 'n' Roll

Sift the flour, bicarbonate of soda and spices into a medium-sized bowl and set aside. Using an electric mixer, beat the remaining butter and sugar for 4 minutes until pale and creamy. Add the treacle, honey and 1 egg, and beat until combined. Add the remaining eggs, one at a time, beating well after each addition. Add a third of the flour mixture to the mixer and beat on a low speed until combined. Add half of the buttermilk and beat well. Repeat this process. Add the remaining third of the flour and beat until thoroughly mixed, but be careful not to overmix because this will toughen the batter.

Pour the cake batter over the pears and bake for 1 hour and 15 minutes or until a fine skewer inserted comes out clean.

Cool in the tin on a wire rack for 15 minutes. If the top of the cake has domed slightly, trim to create a flat surface before turning upside down onto a serving plate. Allow to cool.

To make the vanilla cream, place the seeds in a medium-sized bowl with the cream and icing sugar, and whisk with an electric whisk until soft peaks form.

Serve the vanilla cream alongside the cooled cake.

· · · · · · · · · · ·

'I'M COMING OUT OF MY CAKE
AND I'VE BEEN DOING JUST FINE'

Rock 'n' Roll

KICKSTART MY TART

CARAMELISED SPICED APPLE & THYME TART

A REMIX OF: 'KICKSTART MY HEART' BY MÖTLEY CRÜE, 1989

This Grammy award-winning single, from the album *Dr. Feelgood*, is based on bassist Nikki Sixx's resuscitation following a drug overdose that momentarily rendered him clinically dead. If your main course has almost finished you off, this electrifying cover will get you buzzing.

Serves: 4–6   Preparation time: 10 minutes   Cooking time: 35–40 minutes

3 small Granny Smith apples
60g unsalted butter
seeds from 1 vanilla pod
2 teaspoons thyme leaves, chopped
4 tablespoons caster sugar

¼ teaspoon ground cinnamon
¼ teaspoon mixed spice
1 sheet ready-made puff pastry
1 egg, lightly beaten
whipped cream, to serve

Preheat the oven to 200°C/gas mark 6 and line a baking tray with baking paper.

Peel and core the apples and then cut in half. Cut the halves into 1cm-thick, half moon slices.

Melt the butter in a frying pan over a medium heat and add the vanilla seeds. When the butter begins to foam and bubble, add the apples, thyme, sugar and spices and stir to coat. Continue to cook until the apples start to soften and caramelise. Remove from the heat to cool slightly.

Place the sheet of pastry on the lined baking tray and score a 2cm border around the edge, only cutting halfway through. Arrange the apples inside the pastry border. Reserve any remaining syrup from the pan. Lightly brush the pastry edge with the egg and then place the tray in the oven. Bake for 25–30 minutes or until puffed and golden brown.

Once cooked, spoon the remaining syrup over the top and serve warm with freshly whipped cream.

Rock 'n' Roll

SMELLS LIKE TERRINE SPIRIT

CHAMPAGNE & RASPBERRY TERRINE WITH VANILLA SYRUP

A REMIX OF: 'SMELLS LIKE TEEN SPIRIT' BY NIRVANA, 1991

The defining sound of grunge and anthem for disillusioned youths of the 90s inspires this delicious dish. The song's title gets its name from the 'Teen Spirit' line of female fragrances, hence our yummy dessert is also fruity and aromatic.

Rock 'n' Roll

JELLY TERRINE:

100g caster sugar

500ml champagne or sparkling wine

3½ sheets titanium strength leaf gelatine

250g fresh raspberries

SYRUP:

65g caster sugar

seeds from ½ vanilla pod

Create a narrow parting in the section of hair covering your eyes in order to view your cooking utensils and ingredients.

Combine the sugar and champagne in a medium-sized saucepan and place over a medium-low heat. Stir and bring to a simmer until the sugar dissolves.

Meanwhile, place the leaf gelatine into some cold water to soften for about 5 minutes. Drain and squeeze out the excess water, then add to the hot champagne mixture. Whisk until the gelatine dissolves. Set aside to cool.

Arrange the raspberries on the base of a 900g loaf tin and then pour in enough of the champagne mixture to just cover the raspberries. Cover with clingfilm and refrigerate for about an hour.

Warm up the remaining champagne mixture. Remove the tin from the fridge, take off the clingfilm and pour the champagne mixture over the top. Re-cover and place in the fridge for 4 hours (ideally overnight) to set until firm.

To make the vanilla syrup, put the sugar and 125ml water in a small saucepan. Add the vanilla seeds to the saucepan and stir to combine. Place over a low heat for 3–4 minutes until the sugar dissolves. Once dissolved, increase the heat to high and bring to the boil. Without stirring, boil the syrup for 5 minutes or until it thickens slightly. Set aside to cool until needed.

When you are ready to serve the terrine, briefly dip the base of the loaf tin in boiling water and then invert onto a plate.

Slice the terrine and serve drizzled with the vanilla syrup.

LINE UP

KETCHUP BOYS

RICKY MUTTON

KATY BERRY

NEW SQUIDS ON THE BLOCK

DELI PARTON

BACKSTRAP BOYS

MACKEREL JACKSON

HARRY CONNICK TUNA

MADINNER

NAPKIN COLE

WILSON FILLETS

DESTINY'S CHAI

NICKI FROMAGE

MACAROON 5

DINER ROSS

NELLY FRITTATA

TINA TURNIP
JUSTIN TIMBERLEEK
SIMPLY FED
JUNIPER LOPEZ
CYNDI LOBSTER
THE BEE CHEESE
BOYZ II MENU
LANA DAHL RAY
JOHN MAYO
CELINE DIJON
BRUNO MARZIPAN
**THE ARTIST FORMERLY KNOWN
AS PRUNES**
CROSTINI AGUILERA
MARIAH DAIRY

AND MORE...

CROWD WARMERS

MARKET GREENS WITH LEMON MUSTARD DRESSING

A REMIX OF: 'IT MUST HAVE BEEN LOVE' BY ROXETTE, 1987

If you're broken-hearted, there's no pick-me-up like veggie therapy. This enduring tear-jerker by Sweden's answer to Eurythmics suggests the love is over, but with these yummy greens it's just beginning.

Pop

Serves 2–3   Preparation time: 5 minutes (plus 15 minutes marinating)

1 bunch asparagus, tough white ends
   snapped off
100g rocket (Roxette should also suffice)
1 bunch watercress, stems removed and torn
   into bite-sized pieces
1 firm pear, halved, cored and sliced into
   thin strips
2 tablespoons pumpkin seeds

DRESSING:
2 teaspoons wholegrain mustard
3 tablespoons extra virgin olive oil
2 tablespoons lemon juice
2 teaspoons maple syrup
1 garlic clove, crushed
salt and freshly ground black pepper

Use a vegetable peeler to strip each asparagus stalk into thin ribbons, from the top of the spear to the bottom. Peel as far as you can until you are left with a thin piece, then use a knife to slice this in half. Set aside.

Put all the dressing ingredients in a medium-sized bowl with a pinch of salt and pepper and whisk to combine. Taste and adjust seasoning if necessary. Toss the asparagus with the dressing and leave to marinate for 15 minutes.

Add the rocket, watercress, pear and pumpkin seeds to the bowl, and toss very gently to evenly coat ingredients with the dressing.

Serve as an accompaniment to a main dish or alone as a light starter.

• • • • • • • • • • •

'R-E-C-I-P-E,
FIND OUT WHAT IT MEANS TO ME'

Pop

CLASSIC CAESAR SALAD WITH CRISPY BAGUETTE CROÛTONS

A REMIX OF: 'GET LUCKY' BY DAFT PUNK, 2013

Daft Punk's anthem of 2013 puts the fun in funk and ignites something magical deep in your croûtons. This disco salad will do the same. Daft Punk might prefer a French dressing, but we're insisting on the Italian variety.

Serves: 4   Preparation time: 15 minutes   Cooking time: 30 minutes

SALAD
6 slices prosciutto
4 tablespoons extra virgin olive oil
½ small French baguette, thinly sliced
1 garlic clove, halved
2 baby cos lettuce, leaves separated
4 anchovy fillets (optional)
4 eggs, hard-boiled, peeled and quartered
60g shaved Parmesan

CAESAR DRESSING
1 egg yolk
1 garlic clove, crushed
2 teaspoons Dijon mustard
1 tablespoon lemon juice
2 teaspoons Worcestershire sauce
160ml olive oil
salt and freshly ground black pepper

Preheat the oven to 180°C/gas mark 4 as you do a robotic jive around the kitchen.

Place the prosciutto on a tray lined with baking paper. Bake for 8 minutes or until crisp. Remove from the oven and set aside.

To make the dressing, put the egg yolk, garlic, mustard, lemon juice and Worcestershire sauce in a food-processor and blitz until combined. With the motor running, slowly pour in the olive oil, and blitz until thick and pale. Season with salt and pepper and set aside.

Heat a griddle pan over a high heat. Drizzle the olive oil over both sides of the slices of baguette, and cook on the griddle pan for 2 minutes on each side, or until crisp and golden. Transfer to a plate lined with kitchen paper, and allow any excess oil to drain. Rub the halved garlic evenly across the toasted baguette.

Arrange the lettuce on a platter or bowl and lay over the anchovies, if using. Break large pieces of the prosciutto over the lettuce, and then add the eggs, Parmesan and croûtons, before drizzling the Caesar dressing over the salad. Lightly toss the salad, pop the visor on your helmet and enjoy.

Pop

caprese
in love

HEIRLOOM TOMATO & BOCCONCINI SALAD WITH SALSA VERDE

A REMIX OF: 'CRAZY IN LOVE' BY BEYONCÉ, 2003

Beyoncé's debut single, poignantly titled 'Crazy in Love', saw her partner up with the man she would later marry. And everyone knows that the craziest lovers are the Italians. Therefore this tune has inspired our passionate red, white and green insalata caprese.

Serves: 6   Preparation time: 10 minutes   Cooking time: 10 minutes

1kg heirloom or ripe tomatoes
400g bocconcini balls, roughly torn in half,
    or buffalo mozzarella, torn
crusty bread, to serve (optional)

SALSA VERDE:
30g flat-leaf parsley, leaves only
15g basil leaves
1 garlic clove, finely chopped
2 teaspoons capers, drained
120ml extra virgin olive oil
juice of 1 lemon
salt and freshly ground black pepper

To make the salsa verde, put the parsley, basil, garlic and capers in a food-processor and process until finely chopped. While the processor is running, slowly add the olive oil and lemon juice. Season to taste and continue mixing until all the ingredients are combined. Transfer to a bowl and leave to stand while preparing the salad.

Slice and chop the tomatoes in a variety of ways (sliced, wedges, etc.). Arrange the chopped tomatoes on a platter with the torn bocconcini. Drizzle a little of the salsa verde over each piece of tomato and cheese. Serve immediately, with crusty bread if desired, and do some mean trumpet-aided catwalk power strides back to the kitchen.

Any remaining salsa verde can be refrigerated in an airtight container for a few days.

'Your love's got me cookin' caprese right now.'

Pop

CRISPY NOODLE SALAD WITH TOASTED CASHEWS

A REMIX OF: 'TAKE ON ME' BY A-HA, 1985

This Nordic trio blitzed worldwide charts in '85–'86 with one of the catchiest pop melodies ever and its accompanying revolutionary sketch-animation video clip. It's rumoured their chiselled jaws and cheekbones were the result of eating crunchy Asian salads. Now it's time to give your face bones a workout.

Pop

SALAD:

100g packet egg noodles

vegetable oil, for frying

60g cashews

½ Chinese cabbage, thinly shredded

200g mangetout, tops removed, thinly sliced
on an angle

3 spring onions, thinly sliced on an angle

1 red chilli, thinly sliced on an angle

15g mint leaves, roughly chopped

15g coriander leaves, roughly chopped

80g beansprouts

salt and freshly ground black pepper

DRESSING:

60ml rice vinegar

50g caster sugar

2 tablespoons soy sauce

2 teaspoons sesame oil

60ml groundnut oil

To make the crispy noodles, cook the egg noodles according to the packet instructions and drain very well – they need to be quite dry. Pour enough vegetable oil into a deep, heavy-based pan to come about halfway up the sides and place over a high heat until very hot. Carefully lower in the drained noodles (in batches if necessary). When they rise to the surface, keep frying for a further minute or until crisp and golden. Remove with a slotted spoon and set aside to drain on kitchen paper. Once cool, break into pieces.

Put the cashews in a non-stick frying pan over a medium-high heat. Stir occasionally for 5 minutes or until the cashews become golden and toasted. Remove from the frying pan and set aside to cool.

Put all the ingredients for the dressing in a medium-sized bowl and whisk for a few minutes until the sugar dissolves.

Before you continue, utilise any free worktop space to re-enact synth pop's most famous keyboard riff.

To make the salad, put the shredded cabbage, mangetout, spring onions, chilli and crispy noodles in a large bowl and toss to combine. Add the herbs, beansprouts and cashews and drizzle over the dressing. Season with a little salt and pepper and gently toss until all ingredients are evenly distributed.

Serve immediately.

Pop

COURGETTE & RICOTTA FRITTATA WITH CHERRY TOMATO RELISH

A REMIX OF: 'LITTLE RED CORVETTE' BY PRINCE, 1983

Prince's saucy little number about a one-night stand with a racy woman inspires our equally promiscuous frittata. So drop the top on the 'vette and head out for some drive-thru, or just make it yourself at home.

Serves: 4–6   Preparation time: 15 minutes   Cooking time: 40 minutes (plus cooling time)

5 small courgettes, coarsely grated and squeezed of any excess liquid

6 eggs, lightly beaten

60ml olive oil

100g firm ricotta

40g Cheddar cheese, grated

3 tablespoons finely chopped flat-leaf parsley

½ red chilli, deseeded and finely chopped (optional)

25g butter

salt and freshly ground black pepper

RELISH:

1 tablespoon olive oil

½ red onion, finely diced

1 garlic clove, thinly sliced

250g cherry tomatoes, halved

50g caster sugar

60ml red wine vinegar

To make the relish, heat the olive oil in a small saucepan over a medium heat. Add the onion and a pinch of salt, and gently sweat until softened. Add the garlic and continue to cook for 2 minutes. Add the cherry tomatoes, sugar and vinegar and season with salt and pepper. Mix well, increase the heat to high and bring to the boil, then reduce the heat to medium-high and cook for 8–10 minutes or until the mixture thickens to a jam-like consistency. Remove from the heat and transfer into a small bowl to cool completely.

Preheat the oven to 180°C/gas mark 4. Put the courgettes in a large bowl with the eggs and olive oil. Crumble over the ricotta and Cheddar cheese, and stir to combine. Stir in the parsley and chilli, if using, and then season well with salt and pepper.

Melt the butter in a non-stick, ovenproof frying pan over a medium heat and add the courgette mixture. Cook for 6–8 minutes without stirring, then transfer the pan to the preheated oven and continue to cook for 6–8 minutes or until the egg sets and the top turns golden brown. Leave to cool for 15 minutes before transferring to a serving plate. Serve a slice of warm frittata with the cooled tomato relish and party like it's 1999.

Pop

Little Red Courgette

CHILLI & PRESERVED LEMON MARINATED MOZZARELLA

A REMIX OF: 'I'M LIKE A BIRD' BY NELLY FURTADO, 2000

Nelly Furtado's Grammy-winning first single from her debut album proves that things of good taste can indeed come from Canada (sorry Beliebers). Likewise, good taste is the main theme of our cover version. We're betting you won't be throwing these to the birds.

Serves: 8   Preparation time: 5 minutes   Cooking time: 5 minutes (plus 1 hour marinating)

2 garlic cloves, thinly sliced
30g preserved lemon rind, thinly sliced
1 teaspoon chilli flakes

125ml extra virgin olive oil
4 x 125g buffalo mozzarella balls, sliced
salt and freshly ground pepper

Mix together the garlic, lemon rind, chilli flakes and oil in a small bowl. Season with a little salt and pepper, and set aside.

Drizzle a third of the oil mixture into a large rectangular dish. Place the mozzarella slices in the dish and drizzle over the remaining marinade. Cover (or else they'll 'only fly away') and refrigerate for 1 hour.

When ready to serve, remove the mozzarella from the dish and arrange onto a serving plate or antipasto platter, and drizzle with the remaining marinade.

Pop

Rolling in the Dip

HERBED GOAT'S CHEESE WITH CRUDITÉS

A REMIX OF: 'ROLLING IN THE DEEP' BY ADELE, 2010

This dark and sassy number scooped the 2012 Grammys. And now you can scoop the smooth and pungent dip that it influenced. If there's a perfect guest for these ritzy nibbles it would have to be the ever-elegant Adele.

Serves: 4–6   Preparation time: 10 minutes   Cooking time: 10 minutes

DIP:
155g goat's cheese
125g natural yogurt
1 tablespoon finely chopped dill fronds
1 tablespoon finely chopped flat-leaf parsley
1 teaspoon lemon juice
salt and freshly ground black pepper

CRUDITÉS:
4 large radishes, cleaned and thinly sliced
2 bunches baby carrots, cleaned, trimmed
   and peeled
3 baby beetroots, cleaned and thinly sliced
1 red pepper, deseeded and cut into strips

Put the cheese, yogurt, dill, parsley and lemon juice in a food-processor and blitz until smooth. Season with salt and pepper to taste then transfer to a dipping bowl.

Arrange the radishes, carrots, beetroot and pepper on a platter and serve with the dip.

• • • • • • • • • • •

'I'M PORCINI IN A BOTTLE'

Pop

WINTER SLAW WITH A SPICY PEANUT DRESSING

A REMIX OF: 'LAST FRIDAY NIGHT (T.G.I.F)' BY KATY PERRY, 2011

Need something tasty to mark the end of the working week? Then it's time to get nutty with this vegetarian fusion, inspired by the whimsical American beauty of pop and her tribute to silly alcohol-fuelled Friday nights. Get loose and channel your inner geek.

Pop

¼ savoy cabbage, finely shredded

¼ red cabbage, finely shredded

1 fennel bulb, finely shredded

1 carrot, peeled and julienned (using mandolin or by hand)

½ small beetroot, peeled and julienned (using mandolin or by hand)

1 apple, julienned (using mandolin or by hand)

juice of 1 lemon

3 tablespoons roughly chopped mint leaves

3 tablespoons roughly chopped coriander

salt and freshly ground black pepper

DRESSING:

2 garlic cloves, roughly chopped

3cm piece of ginger, roughly chopped

1 red chilli, roughly chopped

4 tablespoons crunchy peanut butter

1 tablespoon fish sauce

1 teaspoon sesame oil

1 teaspoon runny honey

30ml boiling water

To make the dressing, blend all the dressing ingredients using a blender or hand mixer until smooth. Pour into a bowl or jug.

To make the salad, put both types of cabbage in a large bowl, along with the fennel, carrot, beetroot and apple. Squeeze over the lemon juice and mix well. Season with salt and pepper, and add the herbs and half of the dressing. Toss all the ingredients together well to coat.

Serve the salad by itself, or alongside grilled fish or meat, and drizzle extra dressing over the salad.

· · · · · · · · · · ·

'THEY CALL IT NUTMEG CITY LIMITS'

Pop

HEADLINERS

SOY CHICKEN & PICKLED GINGER WITH SOBA NOODLES

A REMIX OF: 'MAN IN THE MIRROR' BY MICHAEL JACKSON, 1988

'To improve the world, first take a good look at your reflection in the oven door.' This is the true meaning we glean from this massive hit from MJ's seventh solo album *Bad*. Wearing a single white oven mitt, point to the ceiling with one hand, grab your crotch with the other, squeal and commence cooking.

Pop

4 skinless chicken breasts

60ml dark soy sauce

2 tablespoons mirin

1 tablespoon brown sugar

2 teaspoons sesame oil

300g soba noodles

1 Lebanese cucumber, cut into wedges (if you can't find a Lebanese cucumber, ½ an ordinary one will work just as well)

100g pea shoots, trimmed

1 avocado, halved, pitted, peeled and sliced

2 spring onions, thinly sliced on an angle

3 tablespoons roughly chopped coriander

3 tablespoons pickled ginger, chopped

DRESSING:

2 teaspoons caster sugar

80ml ponzu (available from Japanese stores – if you can't find it, try mixing equal parts light soy sauce and Yuzu juice)

2 tablespoons mirin

2 teaspoons fish sauce

juice of 1 lime

1 tablespoon tahini

Put the chicken breasts in a bowl with the soy sauce, mirin, brown sugar and sesame oil. Mix to coat the chicken evenly.

Heat a griddle pan over a high heat or get the barbecue really hot, and cook the chicken for 4–5 minutes on each side or until charred and cooked through. Transfer the chicken to a plate and set aside.

To make the dressing, whisk together all the dressing ingredients in a small bowl and set aside.

Cook the noodles according to the packet instructions. Drain, refresh in cold water, and then drain thoroughly again.

Put the noodles in a large bowl with the cucumber, pea shoots, avocado, spring onions, coriander, pickled ginger and dressing. Divide the salad evenly among the plates. Slice each chicken breast into strips and carefully place on top of the soba noodle salad.

Moonwalk over to your guests and serve immediately.

Pop

CLASSIC TOASTED REUBEN SANDWICHES WITH PICKLED GHERKINS

A REMIX OF: '9 TO 5' BY DOLLY PARTON, 1980

The soundtrack for these pastrami wonders is Dolly Parton's li'l ditty about female rights in the 80s workplace. They're easy enough to make in the kitchen at work and will get you through any gruelling eight-hour shift. Let the hoedown begin.

Serves 6   Preparation time: 10 minutes   Cooking time: 20 minutes

SANDWICHES:
12 slices of rye bread
600g pastrami, thinly sliced from the deli
300g sauerkraut, drained
18 slices Swiss cheese
120g butter
pickled gherkins, to serve
salt and freshly ground black pepper

DRESSING:
250ml mayonnaise
60ml chilli sauce
1 teaspoon Worcestershire sauce
½ teaspoon Tabasco sauce
1 shallot, finely chopped
2 teaspoons grated horseradish

To make the dressing, combine all the dressing ingredients together with a pinch of salt and pepper.

Spread a generous amount of the dressing on six slices of the bread. Top with the pastrami, sauerkraut and cheese, and cover with the remaining slices of bread.

Add 20g of butter into a frying pan over a medium heat. Once the butter melts, add one sandwich and cook for 3 minutes or until golden, before carefully turning over and cooking for a further 2–3 minutes or until toasted and golden. Continue to cook in batches, adding more butter to the pan as needed for each sandwich.

Serve the sandwiches warm with pickled gherkins.

Pop

YOU Can'T CURRY LOVE

THAI GREEN TOFU & VEGETABLE CURRY

A REMIX OF: 'YOU CAN'T HURRY LOVE' BY PHIL COLLINS, 1982

Originally performed in 1966 by Motown pop sensations The Supremes, this song of wise parental advice was later covered by drummer-singer Phil Collins. Like love, just give this curry some time. Good things come to chefs who wait.

Pop

1 tablespoon Thai green curry paste

600ml coconut cream

1 lemongrass stalk, bruised and halved lengthways

1 red pepper, trimmed, deseeded and diced

½ butternut squash, peeled, seeds removed and flesh diced into large chunks

2 kaffir lime leaves, sliced very thinly

120g firm tofu, sliced into cubes

1 large broccoli head, chopped into small florets

125g mangetout, trimmed of stalk

2 tablespoons coriander, roughly chopped

brown rice, to serve

Put a large, wide pan over a medium heat and add the curry paste. Stir for a few minutes or until fragrant. Add the coconut cream, lemongrass, pepper, butternut squash and kaffir lime leaves, and stir to combine. Bring to a simmer, reduce the heat to low and cover.

Cook for 5 minutes, and then stir through the tofu and broccoli florets. Cover the pan again and simmer for a further 5 minutes (adding up to 125ml water if needed).

Add the mangetout and continue to cook gently until all the vegetables are just cooked, stirring often. Once all the vegetables are tender, remove the pan from the heat and remove the lemongrass stalks.

Serve the curry in dishes on top of cooked rice, with a sprinkling of coriander.

• • • • • • • • • • •

'I KISSED A GRILL AND I LIKED IT'

Pop

CALAMARI & LEMON RISOTTO

A REMIX OF: 'KIDS IN AMERICA' BY KIM WILDE, 1981

Kim Wilde was discovered when appearing as a backing vocalist for her brother Ricky. 'Kids in America' became her debut single and she went on to major success. And here we have an Italian dish, set in America and inspired by a Brit. Now that's cosmopolitan cuisine.

Pop

1 litre chicken stock

2 tablespoons olive oil

1 small onion, finely chopped

3 garlic cloves, finely chopped

350g Arborio rice

175ml white wine

500g calamari (squid), cleaned and thinly
sliced

zest of 1 lemon and 1 tablespoon juice

30g Parmesan, grated, plus extra for serving

20g unsalted butter, chopped

250g watercress

salt and freshly ground black pepper

Pour the chicken stock into a small saucepan and place over a medium heat. Heat the stock until it reaches a gentle simmer. Remove from the heat and cover to keep warm.

Place a large non-stick pan over a medium heat. Add the olive oil and onion, and sauté for 1–2 minutes or until softened. Add the garlic and rice, and stir for 2 minutes or until all the grains of rice are coated. Pour in the wine and continue to cook, stirring regularly, until the wine reduces and evaporates completely.

Add one ladleful at a time of the hot chicken stock to the rice. Stir constantly until the stock is absorbed. Repeat this process with the remaining stock, one ladleful at a time, until the rice is nearly cooked (about 15 minutes).

Add the sliced calamari and stir constantly through the rice for 3–5 minutes or until the calamari is just tender. Remove from the heat and stir through the zest of the lemon, a tablespoon of lemon juice, the Parmesan and butter. Season with salt and a generous grind of black pepper.

Divide the risotto between four serving bowls and top with watercress and extra Parmesan. Serve immediately.

SLOW ROAST LEG OF LAMB
WITH CITRUS & THYME

A REMIX OF: '...BABY ONE MORE TIME' BY BRITNEY SPEARS, 1998

Originally written for the Backstreet Boys and TLC, this massive teen pop ballad of the late 90s shot Britney into the Discman of every schoolgirl. Now the roast it inspires could also earn you a gymful of cheerleaders and a prom queen tiara.

Pop

Serves: 4–5   Preparation time: 10 minutes   Cooking time: 5 hours

---

2kg leg of lamb, bone in

3 tablespoons olive oil

3 garlic cloves, crushed

3 sprigs thyme, leaves picked and chopped

1 teaspoon dried oregano

juice of 2 lemons

3 tablespoons roughly chopped flat-leaf
  parsley

salt and freshly ground black pepper

Preheat the oven to 160°C/gas mark 3.

Coat the lamb with the oil, garlic, thyme and oregano. Season generously with salt and pepper. Place the lamb in a deep-sided baking tray, and squeeze over the juice of 1 lemon. Add enough water to the baking tray to reach 2–3cm up the sides.

Transfer the tray to the oven and cook for 3 hours, turning the lamb every hour. Cover with foil and continue to cook for a further 2 hours. Once cooked, remove the lamb from the oven, and allow to rest for 10 minutes.

Carefully transfer the lamb to a serving platter, squeeze over the juice of the remaining lemon, and sprinkle with chopped parsley.

Serve immediately.

Oh, and if you'd like to go back for seconds just 'heat me baby one more time.'

• • • • • • • • • • •

'THEY TRIED TO MAKE ME GO TO RHUBARB AND I SAID "NO, NO, NO"'

Pop

The wiener takes it all

VEAL SCHNITZEL WITH FENNEL & PARMESAN SALAD

A REMIX OF: 'THE WINNER TAKES IT ALL' BY ABBA 1980

As they say, second place is the first loser. Luckily for you, this delicious hammered veal is an ABBAsolute winner. It's a little peculiar that a Swedish supergroup has inspired our take on the national dish of Austria, but let's just put that down to international tastebud diplomacy.

Serves: 8   Preparation time: 15 minutes (plus refrigeration time)   Cooking time: 30 minutes

240g fresh breadcrumbs
10g flat-leaf parsley, chopped
2 tablespoons finely grated lemon zest
100g plain flour, for dusting
2 eggs, lightly beaten
8 thin veal schnitzel steaks
vegetable oil, for shallow frying
salt and freshly ground black pepper

SALAD:
2 tablespoons white wine vinegar
¼ teaspoon sea salt
80ml olive oil
4 baby fennel, very thinly sliced lengthways
400g baby rocket
200g Parmesan, shaved

Put the breadcrumbs, parsley and lemon zest in a shallow bowl and season with salt and pepper. Mix thoroughly to combine.

Put the flour on a medium plate and the egg in a shallow bowl. Lightly dust the veal in the flour, dip into the egg, and then press on the crumb mixture to cover the veal. Lay each schnitzel flat on a tray and refrigerate for 30 minutes.

To make the salad, put the vinegar and sea salt in a serving bowl, and whisk until the salt has dissolved. Gradually add the olive oil, and continue to whisk until the dressing emulsifies. Season with black pepper before adding the fennel, rocket and Parmesan. Toss to combine.

Heat 1cm of vegetable oil in a large frying pan over a high heat. Cook the schnitzels for 1 minute on each side or until golden. Transfer to a plate lined with kitchen paper, and allow any excess oil to drain.

Serve the schnitzels immediately alongside the fennel and Parmesan salad.

Pop

RED WINE-BRAISED VEAL SHANKS

A REMIX OF: 'CALL ME MAYBE' BY CARLY RAE JEPSEN, 2011

You won't be able to stop thinking about these tender, succulent shanks. They're instant crush material. Love at first bite. They share striking similarities with Carly Rae Jepsen's breakthrough tune about instant affection, whose chorus lingers in the mind for an eternity.

Pop

---

2 tablespoons olive oil

50g butter

4 veal shanks (around 2kg in total), French
  trimmed

1 onion, diced

1 carrot, peeled and diced

1 leek, white part only, cut into 2cm rings

2 garlic cloves, chopped

370ml red wine

3 sprigs rosemary

3 sprigs thyme

1 bay leaf

1 litre chicken stock

125ml balsamic vinegar

salt and freshly ground black pepper

green beans or mashed potato, to serve

Don't blush. Just preheat the oven to 180°C/gas mark 4.

Heat the olive oil and half the butter in a large, heavy-based casserole over a medium heat. Once the butter has melted, add the shanks and cook for 5 minutes, turning regularly, to brown on all sides. Remove the shanks from the casserole and set aside.

Add the onion, carrot and leek to the casserole and fry for 6–8 minutes or until the vegetables have softened. Add the garlic and fry for a further 2 minutes. Add the wine, and scrape the bottom of the dish with a wooden spoon to remove all the caramelisation, as this will add great flavour.

Return the shanks to the casserole, bring to the boil, and then simmer for 2 minutes before adding the rosemary, thyme, bay leaf, stock and vinegar. Cover with a piece of baking paper (which fits snugly on top of the mixture), then with a lid, and place the casserole in the oven for 2 hours or until the meat is falling off the bone.

Remove the shanks from the pot, and then strain the sauce through a sieve into a clean pan, pressing the solids to extract all the juices. Put the pan over a medium-high heat and simmer for 15–20 minutes or until the sauce has reduced by half. Once reduced, whisk in the remaining butter and season with salt and pepper to taste.

To serve, pour the sauce over the shanks and serve with green beans or mashed potato.

• • • • • • • • • • •

'COS I'M STROGANOFF TO LIVE WITHOUT YOU'

Pop

Korma Chameleon

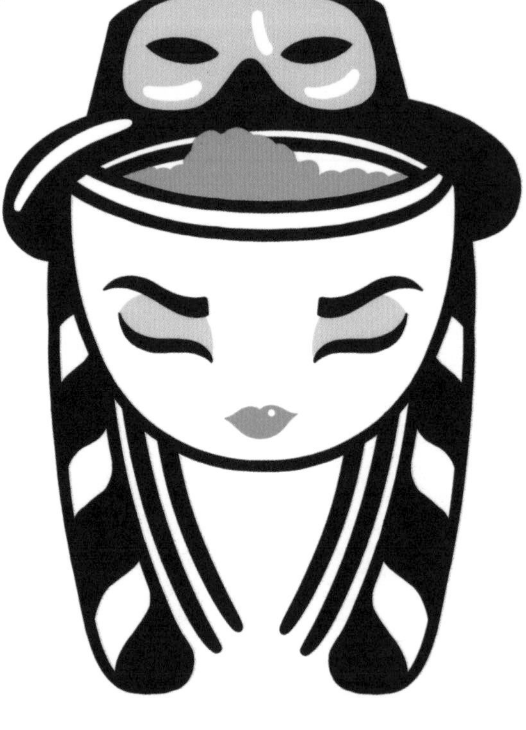

CHICKEN KORMA WITH CUCUMBER & HERB RAITA

A REMIX OF: 'KARMA CHAMELEON' BY CULTURE CLUB, 1983

Do a good deed and karma shall repay you with a fabulous chicken korma. Do another and that korma might transform into a red, green or yellow curry. Well, that's our interpretation of Culture Club's new wave mega hit, which reached the top of the charts in 16 countries. Korma korma korma korma korma chameleon...

Serves: 5–6   Preparation time: 30 minutes (plus marinating time)
Cooking time: 50 minutes

CHICKEN KORMA:
1.5kg chicken breasts, cut into
   bite-sized chunks
5cm piece of ginger, peeled and grated
3 garlic cloves, crushed
150g thick natural yogurt
2 onions, finely chopped
½ teaspoon dried chilli flakes
1 tablespoon vegetable oil
1 tablespoon ground coriander seeds
1 teaspoon turmeric
1 teaspoon garam masala

80g creamed coconut
2 tablespoons ground almonds
salt and freshly ground black pepper

RAITA:
1 Lebanese cucumber, grated (if you can't
   find a Lebanese cucumber, ½ an ordinary
   one will work just as well)
200g natural yogurt
2 tablespoons finely chopped coriander
2 tablespoons finely chopped mint leaves
steamed basmati rice, to serve

Put the chicken, ginger, garlic and yogurt in a large bowl and mix well. Cover and refrigerate to marinate for 12 hours or overnight.

Put the chopped onion and chilli flakes in a food-processor and liquidise until smooth. Set aside.

Heat a large, deep-sided frying pan or cast iron pot over a medium-high heat. Add the oil and once hot, add the ground coriander, turmeric and garam masala. Cook for

CONTINUED OVERLEAF

Pop

1–2 minutes, constantly stirring. Add the onion and chilli paste, and continue to cook for 2 minutes. Add the chicken and any remaining marinade, and cook for a further 8–10 minutes. Add the creamed coconut to the pan and just enough water to cover the chicken. Bring to the boil and stir until the coconut melts into the sauce. Season with salt and pepper and stir the ground almonds into the sauce. Reduce the heat to low and simmer gently for 20–30 minutes or until the chicken is tender.

Meanwhile, remove any excess liquid from the grated cucumber, and place in a small bowl with the yogurt, coriander and mint. Season and stir well. Refrigerate until needed.

Serve the korma with steamed rice and a small spoonful of raita.

• • • • • • • • • • •

'I LOVE THE NIGHTLIFE, I GOT TABBOULEH'

KING PRAWN, PEA & PEARL BARLEY RISOTTO

A REMIX OF: 'SOMEBODY THAT I USED TO KNOW' BY GOTYE FEAT. KIMBRA, 2011

This indie pop tune was a monster hit of the last few years, becoming one of the bestselling digital singles of all time. The dish it inspires is the ultimate comfort food for anyone dealing with a bitter break-up.

Serves: 2   Preparation time: 15 minutes   Cooking time: 30–40 minutes

2 tablespoons olive oil
40g butter
3 garlic cloves, finely chopped
1 leek, finely chopped
200g pearl barley, rinsed
600ml chicken or vegetable stock

150g peas, fresh or frozen
250g raw king prawns, peeled and deveined
small bunch of parsley, roughly chopped
1 lemon
salt and freshly ground black pepper

Place a wide-based saucepan over a medium heat and add the oil and half of the butter. Once the butter melts and begins to foam, add the garlic and leek, and fry gently for 3–4 minutes until the leek softens. Add the pearl barley, stock and 200ml hot water, and simmer for around 20 minutes. Stir often until the barley is nearly cooked, but still has a slight bite to it.

Stir through the peas and prawns, reduce the heat to low and continue to cook for 2–3 minutes or until the prawns are just cooked (add more stock if needed). Remove from the heat, add the chopped parsley and a squeeze of lemon, and season to taste.

Serve immediately.

Pop

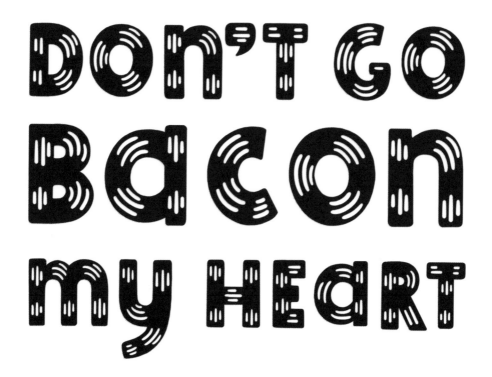

BOSTON BAKED BACON BEANS

A REMIX OF: 'DON'T GO BREAKING MY HEART' BY ELTON JOHN & KIKI DEE, 1976

And now one great duet inspires another. Elton and Kiki, bacon and beans. Heavily influenced by the music of Motown, this US and UK chart-topper provides the perfect soundtrack to a serving of smoky rich beans and lovely crusty toast.

Pop

Serves: 6   Preparation time: 15 minutes   Cooking time: 45 minutes

2 tablespoons olive oil

1 onion, finely chopped

2 garlic cloves, finely chopped

4 rashers bacon, chopped into 2cm pieces

1 carrot, peeled and finely chopped

2 tablespoons tomato purée

1 tablespoon Worcestershire sauce

1 bay leaf

2 sprigs thyme

2 x 400g cans cannellini beans, drained and rinsed

400g can chopped tomatoes

salt and freshly ground black pepper

rustic sourdough toast, to serve

Put a large casserole or wide-based saucepan over a medium heat. Once hot, add the oil, onion, garlic and bacon, and fry until the onion softens and the bacon is lightly golden. Add the carrot and tomato purée, mix well and continue to cook for 1–2 minutes.

Add the Worcestershire sauce, bay leaf, thyme, beans, chopped tomatoes and 120ml water, and then stir to combine. Bring to a gentle simmer, cover the pot with a lid, and then reduce the heat to low. Continue to cook for 35 minutes, stirring occasionally.

Season the beans to taste and serve over hot, buttered sourdough toast.

• • • • • • • • • • •

'THIS IS WHERE I LONG TO BE, LA ISLA FAJITA.'

Pop

PEPPER-SEARED TUNA WITH SOY, SAKE & MIRIN

A REMIX OF: 'SAY MY NAME' BY DESTINY'S CHILD, 2000

If you suspect your man is cheating, he ain't worth a bite of this Asian-inspired fish dish. Get your sisters in the kitchen for some girl power RnB, chuck on this double Grammy winner and spin that lazy Susan.

Pop

TUNA:

½ tablespoon sesame oil

½ teaspoon English mustard

250g fillet of tuna, sashimi quality (trimmed if necessary) and cut to shape into a log of even thickness

2 tablespoons black peppercorns, roughly crushed using a pestle and mortar

1 spring onion, thinly sliced on a sharp angle

DIPPING SAUCE:

25ml sake

½ red chilli, deseeded and finely diced

50ml soy sauce

50ml mirin

To make the dipping sauce, warm the sake in a small saucepan over a medium heat. Add the chilli, soy and mirin, and then remove from the heat and leave to cool.

Mix the sesame oil and mustard in a small bowl. Use a pastry brush to brush the mixture onto the tuna, covering the surface but avoiding the very end. Roll the tuna in the crushed peppercorns to coat the outside.

Harmonise the next chorus while pointing to various kitchen appliances with over-inflated hand gestures.

Heat a dry frying pan over a high heat. Once very hot, add the tuna and cook quickly on all long sides for about 20 seconds, so that the outside sears but the inside remains raw. Remove from the pan and place on a board to cool.

With a sharp knife, cut very fine slices of tuna and lay on a platter. Scatter with spring onion and serve immediately with dipping sauce.

· · · · · · · · · · ·

'EVERYBODY WAS TOFU FIGHTING'

Pop

TOMATO-BRAISED SAUSAGES WITH PARMESAN POLENTA

A REMIX OF: 'SEXYBACK' BY JUSTIN TIMBERLAKE (FEAT. TIMBERLAND), 2006

JT's racy 'SexyBack' marked a new stripped-back, darker, electro sound for the dynamic and talented Timberlake. Turn on the extractor fan. This one is sure to result in polenta of heat in the kitchen.

Serves: 4   Preparation time: 10 minutes   Cooking time: 50 minutes

2 tablespoons olive oil
1kg pork sausages
2 onions, sliced
1 garlic clove, finely sliced
125ml red wine
50ml balsamic vinegar
2 x 400g cans chopped tomatoes
2 tablespoons brown sugar
2 teaspoons dried oregano

3 sprigs thyme
½ teaspoon dried chilli flakes
1.25 litres chicken stock
170g polenta
30g butter
50g Parmesan, finely grated
salt and freshly ground black pepper
2 tablespoons freshly chopped flat-leaf
  parsley, to serve

Heat the olive oil in a large, deep-sided frying pan over a medium-high heat. Add the sausages and cook, turning regularly, for 4–5 minutes or until brown on all sides. Transfer the sausages to a plate and set aside.

Reduce the heat to medium, add the onions to the pan, and cook for 8–10 minutes or until golden. Add the garlic and continue to cook for a further minute. Pour in the wine and vinegar, bring to the boil, and cook for a further 5 minutes or until reduced by half. Add the tomatoes, sugar, oregano, thyme, dried chilli and sausages and season with salt and pepper. Continue to cook, simmering, for 25–30 minutes.

Meanwhile, pour the stock into a medium saucepan and bring to the boil over a medium heat. Gradually add the polenta in a steady stream, and stir until incorporated. Cook for 10–15 minutes or until the polenta thickens, stirring frequently with a wooden spoon. Add the butter and Parmesan, season with salt and pepper, and stir until well combined.

To serve, spoon the sausages and sauce generously over the hot polenta, and finish with a scattering of chopped parsley.

Pop

CHICKPEA & SPINACH CURRY
WITH PAPADUMS

A REMIX OF: 'PAPA DON'T PREACH' BY MADONNA, 1986

This little baby is inspired by the Queen of Pop's classic tune, which deals with the issue of teen pregnancy. And while preventative measures should always be considered, we couldn't find anything regarding abstinence from the delights of Indian cuisine in Madonna's lyrics.

'I need your help cu-rry, please be strong.'

Pop

2 tablespoons groundnut oil

2 teaspoons black mustard seeds

1 teaspoon grated fresh ginger

1 large onion, thinly sliced

1 teaspoon ground cumin

1 teaspoon ground turmeric

1 red chilli, deseeded and finely chopped

3 large ripe tomatoes, roughly chopped

2 x 400g can chickpeas, drained and rinsed

100g baby spinach

salt and freshly ground black pepper

papadums and steamed basmati rice,
    to serve

Heat the oil in a deep frying pan over a medium-high heat. Add the mustard seeds and, as soon as they start to pop, add the ginger, onion and a pinch of salt. Stir and cook for 2 minutes or until the onion softens. Add the cumin, turmeric and chilli, and stir for a further minute.

Add the tomatoes, 125ml water and the chickpeas, and bring to a simmer. Reduce the heat to low, cover and continue simmering for 8–10 minutes. Turn off the heat, add the spinach and a generous seasoning of salt and pepper, and stir until the spinach has wilted.

Serve immediately with papadums and basmati rice.

• • • • • • • • • • •

'WHEN JAMON LOVES A WOMAN'

Pop

FRAGRANT PORK VINDALOO

A REMIX OF: 'VIDEO KILLED THE RADIO STAR', BY THE BUGGLES, 1979

It seems poignant that a song about the innovation of video superseding radio was in fact the first ever music video to be shown on MTV in the USA. It was also the debut single for one-hit wonders the Buggles. But no fancy modern flavours will render our classic vindaloo obsolete.

Pop

2cm piece of ginger, peeled and minced

3 garlic cloves, peeled and finely chopped

2 teaspoons ground cumin

1 teaspoon paprika

2 teaspoons turmeric

¼ teaspoon ground nutmeg

1 teaspoon chilli flakes

1 tablespoon tomato purée

125ml rice vinegar

500g boneless pork shoulder, trimmed and diced

2 tablespoons vegetable oil

1 teaspoon yellow mustard seeds

1 teaspoon ground cinnamon

1 teaspoon cardamom pods, crushed

1 onion, diced

250–375ml chicken stock

basmati or saffron rice, to serve

Blend together the ginger, garlic, cumin, paprika, turmeric, nutmeg, chilli flakes, tomato purée and vinegar in a food-processor (or use a pestle and mortar) until a smooth paste is formed.

Put the diced pork in a medium-sized bowl and add the paste. Stir to coat the pork completely, and then cover with clingfilm and transfer to the fridge to marinate for at least 2 hours.

Heat the vegetable oil in a large, lidded, heavy-based saucepan over a medium heat. Add the mustard seeds, cinnamon and cardamom pods and fry for 1–2 minutes or until the mustard seeds begin to pop. Add the onion and continue to fry for 2–3 minutes or until the onion begins to soften and turn golden.

Add the marinated pork and stir well to combine. Add 250ml chicken stock and bring to a gentle simmer. Reduce the heat to low and cover the saucepan with its lid. Cook for 2 hours or until the pork is tender, adding extra stock if required.

Serve the pork with steamed basmati or saffron rice.

• • • • • • • • • • •

'I HAVE TO BRAISE YOU LIKE I SHOULD'

Pop

ENCORES

MULLED WINE-POACHED PEARS
WITH MASCARPONE

A REMIX OF: 'ALL I WANT FOR CHRISTMAS IS YOU' BY MARIAH CAREY, 1994

Christmas is a time for giving and there ain't no more delicious a gift than this festive gem. Mariah's Christmas classic has inspired our fragrant and spicy punch-themed dessert. So press play and gather around the pear tree.

Pop

MULLED WINE:

zest and juice of 1 orange

zest and juice of 1 lemon

225g caster sugar

4 cloves

1 cinnamon stick

1cm piece of fresh ginger

1 whole nutmeg

1 vanilla pod

750ml red wine

PEARS:

juice of 1 lemon

4 whole pears

200g mascarpone

seeds from 1 vanilla pod

Place all the mulled wine ingredients in a medium-sized saucepan over a medium heat. Bring to the boil, and then reduce the heat to simmer for 10 minutes or until all the sugar has dissolved.

Meanwhile, for the poached pears, put the lemon juice into a bowl of cold water. Peel the pears, and as you peel each pear, place it into the lemon water to prevent it turning brown. Add the whole, peeled pears to the simmering mulled wine, cover with a lid, and simmer for a further 15–20 minutes or until just tender.

While the pears cook, mix the mascarpone with the vanilla seeds and refrigerate until ready to serve.

Remove the pears from the wine and set aside. Bring the wine to the boil, and boil for 10 minutes or until the liquid becomes syrupy. Strain the mulled wine through a sieve into a serving jug.

Serve the warm pears alongside the mascarpone, and finish with a drizzle of the mulled wine syrup.

Warning: Don't be a turkey. Overdo the red wine and Rudolph won't be the only one with a red nose.

• • • • • • • • • • •

'I'M STILL JELLY FROM THE BLOCK'

Pop

PEANUT BUTTER & MILK CHOCOLATE COOKIES

REMIX OF: 'BLAME IT ON THE BOOGIE' BY THE JACKSONS, 1978

The Jacksons made history when their first four singles went to No.1 on the Billboard Hot 100 – an unprecedented rise from peanuts to rolling in dough. Now, speaking of peanuts and rolling dough…

Makes: 24–30   Preparation time: 20 minutes   Cooking time: 25 minutes

120g unsalted butter
170g smooth peanut butter
100g caster sugar
100g soft brown sugar
1 large egg
½ teaspoon vanilla extract

130g plain flour
½ teaspoon salt
¾ teaspoon bicarbonate of soda
150g milk chocolate, chopped into small chunks (or chocolate chips)

Preheat the oven to 160°C/gas mark 3. Line two large baking trays with baking paper and set aside.

Put the butter, peanut butter and both sugars in the bowl of an electric mixer fitted with the paddle attachment. Cream until the mixture becomes light and fluffy. Add the egg and vanilla, and beat until just combined.

Sift the flour, salt and bicarbonate of soda into a separate bowl. Add to the creamed mixture and mix until just combined. Add the chocolate pieces, and stir through.

Roll tablespoonfuls of the mixture into balls and place onto the prepared trays, leaving plenty of space between each one as the dough will spread during baking. Press lightly with a fork. Place the trays in the oven and bake for 15–20 minutes or until the cookies are golden brown. Let the cookies cool on the tray for 10 minutes before transferring them to a wire rack to cool completely.

The cookies can be kept in an airtight container for up to a week.

Pop

BLAME IT ON THE COOKIE

SPICED RAISIN BREAD
& BUTTER PUDDING

A REMIX OF: 'JUST GIVE ME A REASON' BY PINK (FEAT. NATE REUSS), 2013

Never before has there been such an emotional ballad written about a dried grape.

Just give me a raisin,

Just a little bit's enough.

This impassioned account of a couple attempting to rescue a relationship from the brink of collapse won Song of the Year at the 2014 Grammys. And surely if any meal is to rekindle the candles of love it's our spiced-up rendition of the classic bread and butter pudding.

Pop

50g unsalted butter, softened

8 extra-thick slices raisin bread

50g raisins (or sultanas)

600ml double cream

1 teaspoon vanilla extract

4 eggs, plus 4 egg yolks

150g caster sugar

½ teaspoon mixed spice

75g orange marmalade, heated

Preheat the oven to 180°C/gas mark 4.

Spread the butter evenly over each slice of raisin bread. Cut each slice into large cubes (about 3cm). Arrange the bread cubes in a lightly buttered, shallow 1.4 litre baking dish. Sprinkle over the raisins.

Put the cream and vanilla extract in a medium-sized saucepan over a medium heat. Bring to a simmer and set aside for 2 minutes. In a separate bowl, whisk together the eggs, egg yolks, sugar and mixed spice until combined. Pour the hot cream over the egg mixture and whisk until all the ingredients are well combined. Strain through a fine sieve into a large jug, and then pour over the raisin bread. Allow to stand for 15–20 minutes.

Place the baking dish in a large roasting tin, and fill with water to halfway up the sides of the baking dish. Carefully transfer to the oven and cook for 35–40 minutes or until golden brown. Remove the roasting tin from the oven, and then carefully remove the baking dish from the water. Use a pastry brush to brush the top of the pudding with the hot marmalade, and return to the oven for 3–5 minutes. Remove from the oven and allow to rest for 5 minutes before serving.

• • • • • • • • • • •

'GOODBYE MY GUAVA, GOODBYE MY FRIEND'

Pop

SALTED CARAMEL &
CHOCOLATE MOUSSE

A REMIX OF: 'MOVES LIKE JAGGER' BY MAROON 5
(FEAT. CHRISTINA AGUILERA), 2011

For Maroon 5, teaming up with Christina Aguilera sure did seem like an odd duet, but it worked… as does the unexpected chemistry between salty caramel and sweet chocolate. Chuck on some skinny jeans, sing into that whisk and strut your best Mick Jagger.

Serves: 6   Preparation time: 40 minutes   Cooking time: 20 minutes

SALTED CARAMEL:
75g unsalted butter
50g light brown sugar
50g caster sugar
40g golden syrup
125ml double cream
1 teaspoon sea salt flakes

CHOCOLATE MOUSSE:
400g dark chocolate, chopped
40g butter
6 eggs, separated
500ml double cream

To make the caramel, melt the butter, sugars and golden syrup in a small saucepan over a medium heat. Bring to a gentle simmer, and cook for 3 minutes, stirring regularly. Add the cream and salt, and stir to combine. Remove from the heat to cool completely. Get out six 225ml serving glasses, put 2 tablespoons caramel into each, and refrigerate.

To make the mousse, place the chocolate and butter in a small heatproof bowl over a saucepan of simmering water. Stir until the ingredients melt and become smooth. Remove the bowl from the heat, and allow to cool for 5–10 minutes before stirring in the egg yolks. Set aside.

Whisk the cream in a separate bowl until soft peaks form. Use a large metal spoon to gently fold through the chocolate mixture until well combined. Put the egg whites in a separate large bowl and whisk using an electric whisk until soft peaks form. Add half the egg whites to the chocolate mixture, and gently fold the ingredients together. Fold in the remaining egg whites until just combined.

Spoon the mousse over the caramel in the serving glasses. Cover with clingfilm and return to the fridge for 3 hours or until firm. Serve with an extra drizzle of salted caramel.

Pop

WAKE ME UP BEFORE YOUR COCOA

EASY SELF-SAUCING CHOCOLATE PUDDING & COFFEE ICE CREAM

A REMIX OF: 'WAKE ME UP BEFORE YOU GO-GO' BY WHAM!, 1984

This decadent little treat isn't the only thing that's rich. Wham!'s first-ever UK and USA No. 1 single put a few extra zeros in their bank account, which clearly went towards an assortment of fluorescent knits and hair tips. We don't recommend having this one for breakfast. Do the jitterbug.

Pop

ICE CREAM:

300ml double cream

175g condensed milk

2 tablespoons instant espresso powder (or coffee grounds, ground to a fine powder)

2 tablespoons espresso liqueur

PUDDING:

130g self-raising flour

115g cocoa powder, plus 2 tablespoons

200g soft brown sugar

120ml milk

1 egg, lightly beaten

75g butter, melted and cooled slightly

Put all the ingredients for the ice cream in the bowl of an electric mixer fitted with the whisk attachment, and whisk until soft peaks form. Transfer the mixture to a container and freeze for 6 hours or overnight.

To make the pudding, sift the flour and the 2 tablespoons of cocoa into a large bowl, and then add 50g of the brown sugar. Whisk together the milk, egg and butter in a separate bowl. Combine with the dry ingredients, and stir with a wooden spoon until thick and smooth.

Lightly grease a microwave-safe dish, and pour in the pudding mixture. Combine the remaining brown sugar and cocoa in a small bowl, and sprinkle evenly over the batter. Finish by pouring 300ml boiling water over the mixture.

Transfer the dish to the microwave and cook at 500w/50 per cent capacity for 13 minutes. Once cooked, carefully remove from the microwave, cover loosely, and leave to stand for 8–10 minutes. Meanwhile, remove the ice cream from the freezer to soften a little.

And then WHAM! Serve the pudding immediately alongside the coffee ice cream.

· · · · · · · · · · ·

'NEVER GONNA RUN AROUND AND DESSERT YOU'

Pop

GIRLS JUST WANNA HAVE FUDGE

MADELEINES WITH HOT CHOCOLATE SAUCE

A REMIX OF: 'GIRLS JUST WANT TO HAVE FUN' BY CYNDI LAUPER, 1983

Originally written from a male point of view by Robert Hazard, the princess of punk pop tweaked the lyrics and turned this track into a massive girlie anthem. Now we're turning it into a rich, sticky treat. Get all carefree and colourful in the kitchen.

Pop

MADELEINES:

120g butter

3 eggs, at room temperature

1 tablespoon runny honey

100g caster sugar

1 tablespoon soft brown sugar

seeds from 1 vanilla pod

175g plain flour, sifted

1 teaspoon baking powder

SAUCE:

225ml double cream

150g golden syrup

300g dark chocolate (70%), chopped into

small pieces

½ teaspoon coarse salt flakes

Melt the butter in a small saucepan over a low heat. Once completely melted, set aside to cool for 5 minutes.

Whisk the eggs, honey and both sugars in an electric mixer until pale and fluffy. Add half the seeds from the vanilla pod to the mixture (set aside the remaining half for the sauce). Continue to whisk for a further minute. Add the sifted flour and baking powder, and stir through the mixture. Slowly add the melted butter bit by bit, while folding through until just incorporated. Cover the bowl with clingfilm and rest the batter in the fridge for at least 4 hours or overnight.

To make the chocolate sauce, put the cream and golden syrup in a medium-sized saucepan over a medium-high heat. Bring to the boil and stir for 1 minute. Remove from the heat and use a whisk to stir in the chocolate until melted and completely combined. Stir through the reserved vanilla seeds and the salt. Keep warm until ready to use. Alternatively, the sauce can be made the day before, stored in an airtight container, refrigerated and then gently reheated when ready to serve.

Preheat the oven to 180°C/gas mark 4 and grease two 12-hole madeleine trays. Place tablespoonfuls of batter into the prepared moulds. Bake for 8–10 minutes or until golden and cooked through. Remove from the oven and tap out from the tray.

Serve warm or at room temperature and dip generously into the hot chocolate sauce.

Pop

CHERRY & ALMOND CRUMBLE
WITH HONEY YOGURT CREAM

A REMIX OF: 'WRECKING BALL' BY MILEY CYRUS, 2013

Imagine yourself naked and riding a giant cherry as you swing into the kitchen to demolish this recipe. It is only fitting that a crumble be named after the broken walls of Miley Cyrus' 'Wrecking Ball'. While the music video lacks taste, the same can't be said for this yummy dessert.

Pop

CRUMBLE:

800g cherries, pitted and halved

4 tablespoons granulated sugar

1 teaspoon cornflour

juice of 1 lemon

120g plain flour

85g cold unsalted butter, cubed

4 tablespoons caster sugar

4 tablespoons ground almonds

2 tablespoons flaked almonds

CREAM:

300ml double cream

seeds from ½ vanilla pod

300ml natural yogurt

2 tablespoons runny honey

Preheat the oven to 180°C/gas mark 4 and get twerking.

Put the cherries, granulated sugar and 4 tablespoons water in a medium-sized saucepan over a medium-high heat. Bring to the boil and simmer for 10 minutes.

Mix the cornflour in a small bowl with 2 tablespoons of the cherry cooking liquid. Pour the cornflour mixture back into the hot cherries and stir. When the sauce starts to thicken, remove the pan from the heat, and stir in the lemon juice. Transfer the cherries to a 25cm baking dish.

Put the plain flour and butter in a food-processor and blitz until the mixture resembles breadcrumbs. Add the caster sugar and ground almonds and quickly blitz again. Scatter the crumbs, followed by the flaked almonds, over the cherries. Place in the oven and bake for 35 minutes or until the crumble turns golden.

Meanwhile, whip the cream with the vanilla seeds until soft peaks form. Gently stir in the yogurt and honey until combined.

Serve the crumble immediately alongside the yogurt cream.

• • • • • • • • • • •

'WHIP IT, WHIP IT GOOD'

Pop

BANANA, CINNAMON & WALNUT BREAD

A REMIX OF: 'HOW DEEP IS YOUR LOVE' BY BEE GEES, 1977

No amount of facial hair could counter the dominating X chromosomes of perhaps the most successful, and high-pitched, of all brotherly bands, but this manloaf is full of nuts.

Serves: 8   Preparation time: 10 minutes   Cooking time: 1 hour (plus cooling time)

150g unsalted butter, softened, plus extra for greasing
180g caster sugar
3 eggs
3 large ripe bananas (350g), mashed
110ml buttermilk
1 teaspoon vanilla extract
1 teaspoon bicarbonate of soda
½ teaspoon salt
½ teaspoon ground cinnamon
350g plain flour
100g walnuts, roughly chopped

Preheat the oven to 180°C/gas mark 4. Grease a 900g loaf tin with butter and line the base with baking paper.

Use an electric mixer or hand-whisk to beat the butter and sugar for 4–5 minutes or until light and fluffy. Add the eggs, one at a time, beating well after each egg. Add the bananas, buttermilk and vanilla, and mix until just combined. Add the bicarbonate of soda, salt, cinnamon and flour, and fold through with a spatula until the batter is mixed together (be careful not to overmix). Add the walnuts and gently stir through the batter.

Pour the batter into the prepared loaf tin and bake for 45 minutes or until a skewer inserted comes out clean. Remove it from the oven and leave to cool in the tin for 30 minutes before transferring to a wire rack to cool completely.

Serve sliced and buttered, either warm or at room temperature.

Pop

LINE UP

PLUM DMC

C+C MUESLI FACTORY

FEASTIE BOYS

LUPE TABASCO

ENTREE3000

SIR MIX SHALLOT

MC HAMPER

FISHY SCENT

CYPRUS DILL

CHAKA CORN

FRUITS MANUVA

VANILLA SLICE

DUKKAH DRE

TIMBERLAMB

CRESS BROWN

THE NOTORIOUS BLT

CYPRUS DILL
WONTON CLAN
BIG DADDY CAYENNE
CREAM LATIFAH
LIMP BRISKET
**CHICKEN AND SWEET
CORN SNOOP**
HALAL COOL J
MISO ELLIOT
BEL BIV DEVOUR
TINIE TEMPEH
NAUGHTY BY NACHO
EGGZIBIT
KANYE ZEST
PEA DIDDY

AND MORE...

CROWD WARMERS

INSANE IN THE BRINE

WARM CHILLI & CITRUS
SPICED OLIVES

A REMIX OF: 'INSANE IN THE BRAIN' BY CYPRUS HILL, 1993

These crazy hip hop nibbles will drive your tastebuds loco.

If you're looking to satisfy the munchies, you can't go past these dope hors d'oeuvres, inspired by this major crossover hit from the same guys who brought you 'Hits From the Bong'. Grab a cocktail stick and go nuts.

Hip Hop & RnB

125ml extra virgin olive oil

3 garlic cloves, peeled and smashed

1 red chilli, thinly sliced

3 slices of orange rind, pith removed

3 slices of lemon rind, pith removed

1 tablespoon rosemary leaves

¼ teaspoon allspice

100g Kalamata olives, pitted

100g Sicilian olives, pitted

Heat the olive oil, garlic and chilli in a small saucepan over a medium-low heat. Heat gently for 4–5 minutes or until the garlic begins to turn golden. Add the orange rind, lemon rind, rosemary and allspice, and continue to heat for a further minute. Add the olives and stir to combine. Remove from the heat, allow to cool, and transfer to the fridge to marinate for 4 hours (or up to a week).

To serve, gently reheat the olives in a small saucepan over a medium heat for 2–3 minutes.

• • • • • • • • • • •

'SORRY MISS JACKSON, I ATE YOUR VEAL'

Hip Hop & RnB

CRISPY SAFFRON ARANCINI BALLS

A REMIX OF: 'I BELIEVE I CAN FLY' BY R. KELLY, 1996

It seems fitting that one cheesy number should inspire another. This snack is influenced by the modern titan of RnB and his tale of motivation and self-belief. There is no ceiling on human endeavour, nor on these delicious treats.

Serves: 4–5   Preparation time: 15 minutes
Cooking time: 40–50 minutes (plus cooling time)

2 tablespoons olive oil
20g butter
1 onion, finely chopped
1 celery stick, finely chopped
pinch of saffron
250g Arborio rice
650ml chicken or vegetable stock, warmed
40g Parmesan, grated
vegetable or olive oil, for frying

80g bocconcini, halved or quartered into small bite-sized pieces (or buffalo mozzarella)
50g plain flour
2 eggs, lightly beaten
100g panko breadcrumbs
salt and freshly ground black pepper
1 lemon, sliced, to serve

Heat the oil and butter in a large saucepan over a medium heat. Add the onion, celery and saffron and cook, stirring constantly, for 5 minutes or until the vegetables soften. Add the rice to the pan and stir to coat the grains in the oil and butter. Add the warm stock, cover with a lid and simmer gently, stirring occasionally, for 15–20 minutes or until the rice is al dente. Add the grated Parmesan, season with salt and pepper and stir through until the cheese melts. Pour into a tray and refrigerate for 20 minutes.

Preheat the vegetable oil in a deep-fat fryer or large saucepan until it reaches 175°C.

Using damp hands (to prevent sticking), shape a tablespoonful of the cooled rice into a ball. Push a little piece of bocconcini into the centre and roll again to enclose it. Repeat with the remainder of the rice and cheese. You should end up with 18–20 balls.

Roll the balls of rice first in the flour, followed by the egg and then finally the panko, making sure to shake off any excess. Deep-fry the balls in batches until they are crisp and golden brown. Remove from the oil and drain on kitchen paper.

Serve with a slice of lemon.

Hip Hop & RnB

LET'S GET A STARTER

BEETROOT CARPACCIO WITH GOAT'S FETA, TOASTED WALNUTS & BABY HERBS

A REMIX OF: 'LET'S GET IT STARTED' BY THE BLACK EYED PEAS, 2004

Originally released as 'Let's Get Retarded', this eventual Grammy winner was only reworked for use as a promo for the 2004 NBA Playoffs, but became so popular it was rereleased under the new title. Our yummy vegetarian appetiser will be just as popular.

Serves: 4–6   Preparation time: 15 minutes   Cooking time: 30 minutes (plus cooling time)

400g beetroot (about 4–5), trimmed
750ml red wine vinegar
200g caster sugar
5 sprigs thyme
1 large piece of orange rind

60g walnuts, toasted and roughly chopped
60g soft goat's milk feta
extra virgin olive oil, to drizzle
50g baby herbs (mint, basil, etc)
salt and freshly ground black pepper

Put the beetroot, vinegar, sugar, thyme and orange rind in a large saucepan with 1 litre water and mix to combine. Bring to the boil over a medium-high heat, reduce the heat and simmer for 20–25 minutes or until the beetroot is just tender when tested with a sharp knife. Drain the beetroot and set aside to cool.

When completely cool, peel and thinly slice the beetroot using a mandolin slicer and arrange on a serving platter.

Scatter over the walnuts, dot with the feta and drizzle generously with the extra virgin olive oil. Scatter over baby herbs and season with salt and pepper. Serve immediately.

Hip Hop & RnB

LOVE THE WAY YOU LIME

ROAST PUMPKIN, CHICKPEA, PISTACHIO & LIME QUINOA

A REMIX OF: 'LOVE THE WAY YOU LIE' BY EMINEM FEAT. RIHANNA, 2010

This zesty, crunchy salad is inspired by Eminem and Rihanna's bestselling single. The song is based on the difficulties of love-hate relationships. Our cover is purely love–love.

Serves: 6–8   Preparation time: 20 minutes   Cooking time: 50 minutes

1kg pumpkin, peeled, seeds removed and
  flesh cut into 3cm pieces
2 tablespoons olive oil
1 teaspoon ground cumin
1 teaspoon ground coriander
170g quinoa, rinsed
40g pistachios, roughly chopped

400g can chickpeas, drained and rinsed
zest and juice of 1 lime
150g feta, crumbled (optional)
3 tablespoons chopped flat-leaf parsley
3 tablespoons roughly chopped mint
2 tablespoons extra virgin olive oil
salt and freshly ground black pepper

Preheat the oven to 200°C/gas mark 6 and line a baking tray with baking paper. Put the pumpkin, oil, cumin and coriander in a large bowl and toss to coat. Spread the pumpkin evenly over the tray and season well with salt and pepper. Roast for 40–45 minutes until golden brown and tender. Remove and cool to room temperature.

Fill a large saucepan with water and add the quinoa. Place over a medium-high heat and bring to the boil. Boil rapidly for 8–10 minutes or until just tender (not mushy). Drain, then transfer to a large bowl to cool, fluffing gently with a fork from time to time.

Once cool, add the roast pumpkin and remaining ingredients. Season generously and gently toss to combine. Serve alone or as an accompaniment to grilled fish or meat.

Hip Hop & RnB

TRUFFLE, MUSHROOM
& GARLIC BRUSCHETTA

A REMIX OF: 'FUNKY COLD MEDINA' BY TONE LŌC, 1989

Tone Lōc's classic platinum single (written by Young MC) tells the story of a man who uses an aphrodisiac love potion in a bid to improve his chances with the ladies. You'll also fall under the spell of our little delight, but perhaps go easy on the garlic if you've got similar motives.

Hip Hop & RnB

1 tablespoon olive oil

20g unsalted butter

500g mixed mushrooms (such as chestnut, button and flat mushrooms), sliced

2 garlic cloves, finely chopped

125ml dry white wine

125ml chicken stock

1½ tablespoons truffle oil

2 tablespoons roughly chopped flat-leaf parsley

2 thick slices of rustic sourdough

salt and freshly ground black pepper

Heat the oil and butter in a large frying pan over a medium-high heat. When the butter melts and starts to foam, add the mushrooms and cook, stirring occasionally, for 3–4 minutes or until the mushrooms are wilted and starting to colour. Add the garlic and sauté for 1 minute.

Reduce to a medium heat, add the wine and simmer for 2–3 minutes or until most of the wine is absorbed. Add the chicken stock and cook, stirring often, for 15 minutes or until most of the liquid is absorbed.

Remove the frying pan from the heat and stir in the truffle oil and parsley. Season well with salt and pepper. Cover to keep warm.

Heat a ridged griddle pan over a high heat. Toast the slices of sourdough for 2–3 minutes on each side or until the bread is toasted with charred griddle marks.

Put the toasted sourdough on serving plates and top generously with the warm truffle mushrooms. Serve immediately.

• • • • • • • • • • •

'YO STOP. COAGULATE & THICKEN'

Hip Hop & RnB

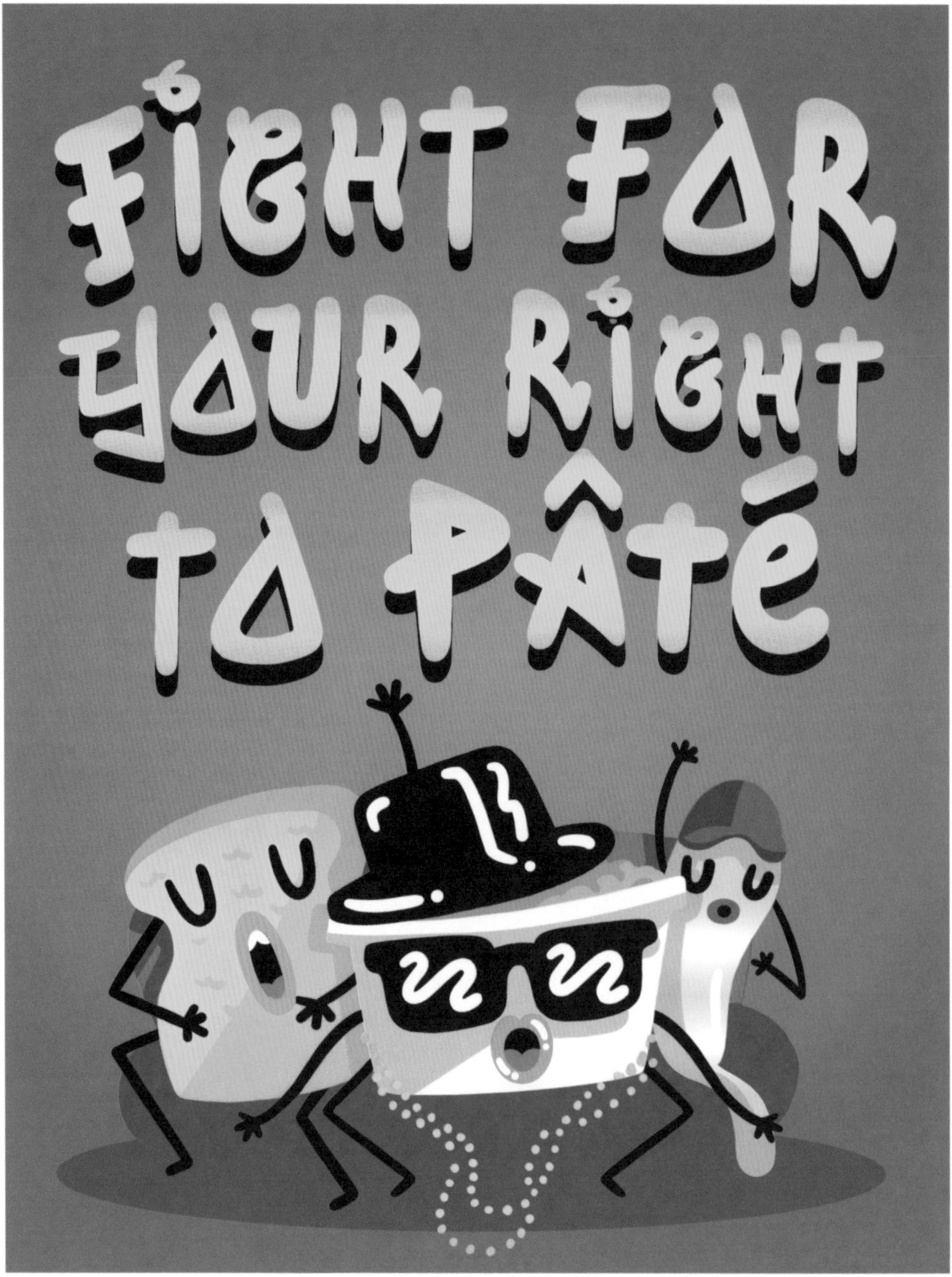
FIGHT FOR YOUR RIGHT TO PÂTÉ

PÂTÉ & CARAMELISED ONION TOAST SOLDIERS

A REMIX OF: '(YOU GOTTA) FIGHT FOR YOUR RIGHT (TO PARTY!)'
BY THE BEASTIE BOYS, 1987

Intended as a cheeky parody of party songs of the time, this ripper from the Beastie Boys ironically went on to become an anthem amongst those it was attempting to mock. Now it inspires fancy pants party food. Start by gatecrashing the kitchen and crushing your mum's glasses with your L.A Gears. Kick it!

Serves: 4   Preparation time: 10 minutes   Cooking time: 1 hour 15 minutes

50ml olive oil

3 red onions, thinly sliced

3 garlic cloves, finely chopped

1 tablespoon brown sugar

1 tablespoon red wine vinegar

100g chicken liver pâté

8 slices white bread, crusts removed

50g butter, just melted

Heat the oil in a large saucepan over a low heat. Add the onions and stir occasionally for 45 minutes until very tender and caramelised. Add the garlic and continue to cook for a further 5 minutes. Stir through the brown sugar and red wine vinegar and cook for another 5 minutes or until the liquid reduces. Season to taste and set aside to cool.

Put the pâté in a medium-sized bowl and use a metal spoon to mix well until it softens to a spreadable consistency. Spread the pâté over four of the slices of bread and then carefully top with the caramelised onions.

Cover the onions with the remaining slices of bread to make four sandwiches.

Heat a griddle pan over a high heat. Use a pastry brush to carefully spread just melted butter on the two outer sides of each sandwich, then cook each for 1 minute on both sides or until golden. Place the sandwiches on a board and slice each into four soldiers.

Serve as canapés or as a starter.

HERE COMES THE HOT PEPPER

CHARGRILLED SWORDFISH WITH SMOKY PEPPER SALAD

A REMIX OF: 'HERE COMES THE HOTSTEPPER' BY INI KAMOZE, 1994

If you consider yourself a lyrical gangsta, get your rhyming gear around this chronic dish. This Ini Kamoze killer blend of reggae and hip hop reached the top spot on the US charts in '94, so we created our smoky swordfish composition in its honour. All this talk of yumminess is Jamaican me hungry...

Hip Hop & RnB

2 large red peppers

1 garlic clove, finely chopped

1 lemon, one half juiced, the other half cut
  into wedges to serve

5 tablespoons extra virgin olive oil

400g can chickpeas, rinsed and drained

2 tablespoons capers, rinsed and drained

2 swordfish fillets

4 tablespoons freshly chopped
  flat-leaf parsley

salt and freshly ground black pepper

Char the peppers over an open gas flame or on a barbecue hot plate for 8 minutes or until black and blistered all over (use a pair of tongs to turn regularly). Once blackened, put the peppers in a large bowl, cover with clingfilm and leave for 10 minutes before peeling off the skin from each one.

Use a knife to core and deseed the peppers, and then slice the flesh into thin strips. Put the strips into a medium-sized bowl and add the garlic, 2 tablespoons of lemon juice, 3 tablespoons of olive oil, the chickpeas and capers. Season with salt and pepper. Stir well to combine, and then set aside to marinate.

Place the swordfish fillets onto a plate, drizzle each side with the remaining olive oil, and season with salt and pepper. Heat a large chargrill pan or barbeque over a high heat. Place the swordfish onto the grill and cook for 3-4 minutes on each side, turning once.

Once the fish is cooked through, transfer to serving plates and serve alongside the pepper salad.

Scatter with chopped parsley and serve with a wedge of lemon.

· · · · · · · · · · ·

'I'VE GOT THE FLOUR!'

Hip Hop & RnB

ROAST TURKEY, BACON, ROCKET & TORN BREAD SALAD

A REMIX OF: 'IN DA CLUB', BY 50 CENT, 2003

One of the most popular hip hop songs of the modern era has inspired our delicious spin on the club sandwich. It's evident when looking at 50 Cent in the music video that it's not just the bread in this salad that's ripped.

Serves: 4   Preparation time: 20 minutes   Cooking time: 20 minutes

2 bread rolls, torn into bite-sized pieces
2 tablespoons olive oil
3 bacon rashers
100g rocket leaves
1 avocado, halved, pitted, peeled and diced
200g cherry tomatoes, halved
500g roast turkey, shredded

DRESSING:
80ml buttermilk
3 tablespoons mayonnaise
2 tablespoons apple cider vinegar
1 spring onion, finely sliced
salt and freshly ground black pepper

Preheat the oven to 200°C/gas mark 6 and line two baking trays with baking paper.

Spread out the torn bread on one tray and d-rizzle with olive oil. Toss to coat. Lay out the bacon rashers on the second tray. Put both trays in the oven for 10 minutes or until the bread is golden brown and the bacon is crispy. Set aside.

Whisk together the buttermilk, mayonnaise, vinegar and spring onion in a large bowl. Season with salt and pepper. Add the rocket, avocado, tomatoes, toasted bread and turkey, and toss gently to coat with the dressing. Break up the crispy bacon into large bite-sized pieces and sprinkle over the salad.

Serve immediately with a bottle full of bub and party like it's your birthday.

IN DA CLUB SANDWICH

STRAIGHT CHOWDER COMPTON

CAULIFLOWER & SMOKED HADDOCK CHOWDER WITH BROKEN BISCUITS

A REMIX OF: 'STRAIGHT OUTTA COMPTON' BY N.W.A, 1988

This pioneer of gangsta rap is the lead single from N.W.A.'s album of the same name. A tale of gang tussles with the boys in blue, it inspires this hellraising bowl of creamy goodness. Soup this good should be illegal.

Serves: 6   Preparation time: 15 minutes   Cooking time: 40 minutes

4 smoked haddock fillets, approximately 140g per fillet, skinned

1 litre milk

60g butter

2 leeks, thinly sliced

4 shallots, thinly sliced

4 bacon rashers, chopped into 2cm pieces

2 swedes, diced into 2cm pieces

1½ cauliflower heads, broken into large florets

salt and freshly ground black pepper

12 water biscuits, broken into pieces, to serve

Put the haddock and milk in a medium-sized saucepan over a medium-high heat. Bring to the boil, reduce the heat and set aside for 10 minutes to infuse.

Melt the butter in a large saucepan over a medium-high heat. Add the leeks, shallots and bacon, and stir for 2–3 minutes or until the leek begins to soften. Add the swede and cauliflower and continue to stir for a further 3–4 minutes.

Pour the haddock and milk mixture over the vegetables and bring to the boil, then reduce the heat to low and simmer for 15 minutes or until the vegetables are just tender. Break up any large pieces of haddock with a wooden spoon. Season with salt and pepper to taste, and serve with the water biscuits crumbled over the top.

Hip Hop & RnB

SO FISH SO CLEAN

WARM NEW POTATO & MACKEREL SALAD

A REMIX OF: 'SO FRESH, SO CLEAN' BY OUTKAST, 2001

This cheeky track by perhaps the most dynamic of musical duos inspires our fresh and zesty delight. The music video features cameos by TLC and Ludacris, among others. Our salad features appearances by cress, parsley and lemon.

Serves: 2   Preparation time: 10 minutes   Cooking time: 30 minutes

350g new potatoes
100g crème fraîche
1 teaspoon horseradish, grated (or use creamed horseradish if fresh isn't available)
juice of 1 lemon

200g smoked mackerel fillets, skinned and flaked
85g watercress
1 tablespoon chopped flat-leaf parsley
salt and freshly ground black pepper

Fill a large saucepan with slightly salted water, add the potatoes and set over a medium-high heat. Bring to the boil, reduce the heat to medium and simmer for 10 minutes or until tender. Drain, cut the potatoes in half and set aside to cool for 5 minutes.

Meanwhile, mix together the crème fraîche, horseradish and lemon juice in a large bowl, and season with pepper. Add the warm potatoes to the dressing and toss to coat. Add the mackerel, watercress and parsley, and gently combine. Serve immediately.

'Ain't no salad dope as me, I'm just so fish, so clean.'

Hip Hop & RnB

DON'T BAY LEAF THE HYPE

PUY LENTIL SALAD WITH CRISPY BACON

A REMIX OF: DON'T BELIEVE THE HYPE, BY PUBLIC ENEMY, 1988

Let's pump up the legume. This truly def pulse salad is a tribute to the equally tasty Public Enemy tune that inspired it. The politically charged lyrics were a protest about the band's alleged mistreatment in the media. And they're right; don't believe everything you read – unless it's these helpful steps to a world of Flavor Flav.

Hip Hop & RnB

460g Puy lentils, rinsed and drained

2 fresh bay leaves

1 tablespoon olive oil

4 rashers bacon, sliced into strips

1 red onion, finely chopped

160g currants

30g walnuts, toasted and roughly chopped

4 tablespoons capers, drained

3 tablespoons freshly chopped parsley

3 tablespoons freshly chopped mint

DRESSING:

80ml extra virgin olive oil

60ml cider vinegar

1 tablespoon maple syrup

1 tablespoon Dijon mustard

1 teaspoon ground cumin

½ teaspoon ground coriander

¼ teaspoon cayenne pepper

½ teaspoon mixed spice

salt and freshly ground black pepper

Put the lentils and bay leaves in a medium-sized saucepan and cover with cold water (3–4cm above the lentils). Bring to the boil over a medium heat. Reduce the heat to a simmer and cook for 15–20 minutes or until just al dente (be careful not to overcook!). Drain the lentils and set aside to cool slightly.

Heat the olive oil in a large frying pan over a medium-high heat. Add the bacon and fry for 4–5 minutes or until golden and crispy. Transfer to a plate lined with kitchen paper to absorb any excess oil. Set aside.

To make the dressing, put all the dressing ingredients in a bowl. Season with salt and pepper, and whisk vigorously to combine.

Tip the warm lentils into a large bowl and stir in the bacon strips, red onion, currants, walnuts and capers. Pour over the dressing and stir to combine. Sprinkle in the herbs and season with salt and pepper to taste.

Serve slightly warm or at room temperature.

HEADLINERS

BLURRED LOINS

ROAST PORK LOIN WITH CIDER & APPLE SAUCE

A REMIX OF: 'BLURRED LINES' BY ROBIN THICKE (FEAT. T.I. & PHARRELL), 2013

Robin Thicke's steamy yet controversial collaboration with Pharrell and T.I. became 2013's biggest chart hit and one of the most downloaded songs ever. Just don't get too heavy-handed with the cider, otherwise you might end up singing blurred lines.

Hip Hop & RnB

8 sage leaves, chopped

zest of 1 lemon

2.5kg piece of pork loin, boned and
    fat scored

2 red onions, quartered

salt and freshly ground black pepper

SAUCE:

500g Granny Smith apples, peeled, cored
    and chopped

30g butter

3 tablespoons cider

25g brown sugar

Preheat the oven to 230°C/gas mark 8.

Rub the sage and lemon zest over the pork and season generously with salt and pepper. Put the onions into a large roasting tray and rest the pork on top. Transfer the roasting tray into the oven and roast for 30 minutes, and then reduce the heat to 160°C/gas mark 3. Continue to roast, basting regularly, for 90–120 minutes or until the pork is cooked through and the crackling is crisp.

Meanwhile, to make the apple and cider sauce, heat the apples, butter, cider and 3 tablespoons water in a medium-sized saucepan over a medium-low heat. Bring to a simmer, cover with a lid, and reduce the heat to low. Continue to cook for 5 minutes or until the apples have softened. Add the brown sugar and stir until it dissolves in the hot mixture. Set aside.

Once the pork is cooked, allow to rest for 10 minutes before carving into thick slices.

Serve alongside the cider and apple sauce.

THiS iS HOW We CHeW it

GRILLED CAJUN CHICKEN FAJITAS WITH HOMEMADE SALSA

A REMIX OF: 'THIS IS HOW WE DO IT' BY MONTELL JORDAN, 1995

This catchy number spent seven weeks at No. 1 in the USA. And now Montell's helping to put the rap in wrap with these tasty tortillas. Montell went on to become a church worshipper, which is fitting as these fajitas are heaven-sent.

Hip Hop & RnB

Serves: 4   Preparation time: 15 minutes   Cooking time: 15 minutes

---

FAJITAS:

2 chicken breasts, skin removed, sliced into
2cm-thick strips

2 teaspoons smoked paprika

1 teaspoon ground cumin

1 red pepper, trimmed and sliced into
1cm strips

1 red onion, thinly sliced

3 tablespoons olive oil

salt and freshly ground black pepper

SALSA:

300g cherry tomatoes, quartered

2 shallots, finely chopped

1 red chilli, finely chopped

1 small bunch of coriander, leaves removed
and roughly chopped

zest and juice of 1 lime

2 tablespoons extra virgin olive oil

TO SERVE:

8–10 flour tortillas, heated to packet
instructions

1 avocado, halved, pitted, peeled and sliced

Cheddar cheese, grated

To make the fajita filling, put the chicken strips in a medium-sized bowl along with the spices, pepper, onion, olive oil and a pinch of salt and pepper. Mix well to coat the chicken with oil and spices. Set aside to marinate for 5 minutes.

Put all the ingredients for the salsa in another medium-sized bowl, season well and stir to combine. Set aside.

Preheat a griddle pan over a high heat or a hot barbecue. Once hot, add the chicken and vegetables to the pan and, stirring occasionally, grill for 6–8 minutes or until the chicken is cooked and golden brown.

Divide the warm tortillas between serving plates and top with the chicken, pepper and onion mix. Spoon over the salsa, and add a few slices of avocado and a sprinkle of grated cheese. Fold to enclose the filling.

Hip Hop & RnB

HOLY QUAIL

ROASTED QUAIL WITH LEMON TABBOULEH

A REMIX OF: 'HOLY GRAIL' BY JAY Z (FEAT. JUSTIN TIMBERLAKE), 2013

Jesus may have turned water into wine, but what about the dish to accompany it? For your last supper, feast on this. The Holy Grail of dinners is inspired by Jay Z's track about his love-hate relationship with fame.

Serves: 4   Preparation time: 20 minutes (plus 20 minutes soaking)
Cooking time: 15 minutes

4 quail
2 tablespoons olive oil
2 tablespoons sumac
zest and juice of 1 lemon, plus extra wedges
   to serve
salt and freshly ground black pepper

TABBOULEH:
85g bulgar wheat
2 bunches of flat-leaf parsley, finely chopped
1 small bunch of mint, leaves picked, finely
   chopped
2 small tomatoes, diced into 1cm pieces
80ml extra virgin olive oil

Tip the bulgar wheat into a medium-sized bowl and cover with boiling water. Set aside for 15–20 minutes or until just softened.

Preheat the barbecue or grill to a high heat.

Use a sharp knife to cut each quail through the breastbone, and flatten out the bird with the palm of your hand. Carefully score down each side of the spine and remove the backbone. Brush each quail with the olive oil and sprinkle over the sumac and lemon zest. Season with salt and pepper. Set aside to marinate while you make the tabbouleh.

Once the bulgar wheat is tender, tip into a sieve and drain off any excess liquid. Transfer to a large bowl, add the herbs, tomatoes and lemon juice, and stir to combine. Add the extra virgin olive oil and season with salt and pepper to taste. Set aside.

Cook the quail on the barbecue or hot grill, skin-side down, for 5 minutes. Turn over and grill for a further 5 minutes or until golden and crisp on the outside and cooked through.

Drizzle an extra squeeze of lemon over the quail, and serve immediately alongside the lemon tabbouleh. Enjoy with a chalice of dry white wine.

Hip Hop & RnB

BLACK PEPPER CRAB

A REMIX OF: 'WALK THIS WAY' BY RUN-DMC (FEAT. AEROSMITH), 1986

We're breathing new life into this classic dish, which takes us to the epic tune that provides its soundtrack. Although the original song was released by Aerosmith, it was the Run-DMC collaboration 11 years later that catapulted hip hop into the mainstream charts and paved the way for the Rap Rock genre... or is that Rap Wok?

Serves: 2   Preparation time: 10 minutes   Cooking time: 15 minutes

1kg cooked whole crabs, cleaned, dead man's fingers and stomach sac removed, and chopped into four with the back shell removed
1 teaspoon ketjap manis
1 teaspoon palm sugar
3 tablespoons vegetable oil

15 fresh curry leaves
3 garlic cloves, peeled and finely chopped
3cm piece ginger, peeled and grated
4 spring onions, thinly sliced on an angle
1 tablespoon black peppercorns, coarsely crushed
15g unsalted butter

Start by preparing the crabs (or you can ask your fishmonger to prepare them for you).

Combine the ketjap manis, palm sugar and 60ml water in a small bowl. Set aside.

Place a large wok over a very high heat. Once the wok begins to smoke, add the vegetable oil, along with the curry leaves, garlic, ginger and three-quarters of the spring onions. Fry for 1 minute or until the onions turn light golden. Add the peppercorns, crab, and ketjap manis mixture. Fry for a further 3–4 minutes or until the crab has warmed through. Remove from the heat and stir through the butter.

Serve immediately, sprinkled with the remaining spring onions.

Hip Hop & RnB

THRIFT CHOP

PAPPARDELLE WITH RUSTIC ROCKET PESTO

A REMIX OF: 'THRIFT SHOP' BY MACKLEMORE & RYAN LEWIS (FEAT. WANZ), 2012

Are you a thrift-shopping hobo hipster who likes their clothes pre-worn but their food fresh? Lettuce introduce you to our rocket and basil dedication to this catchy anthem about canny spending. It's simply a case of some inexpensive fresh ingredients, a food-processor and ... hey pesto!

Serves: 4   Preparation time: 15 minutes   Cooking time: 10–15 minutes

120g baby rocket

15g basil leaves

40g Parmesan, grated, plus extra to serve

100g pine nuts, toasted

2 garlic cloves, chopped

125ml extra virgin olive oil

1 tablespoon lemon juice

400g pappardelle

salt and freshly ground black pepper

Put the rocket, basil, Parmesan, pine nuts and garlic in a food-processor and process until roughly chopped (be careful not to over-process as you want the pesto to remain quite chunky). With the motor running, gradually add the oil in a thin, steady stream until well combined. Stir in the lemon juice, and season with salt and pepper to taste. Set aside.

Cook the pasta in a large saucepan of boiling water according to the packet instructions or until al dente. Drain well and return to the pan. Add the pesto and gently toss to combine.

Serve immediately with an extra grating of Parmesan.

Hip Hop & RnB

MISO & SHIITAKE RAMEN

A REMIX OF: 'NO WOMAN, NO CRY' BY BOB MARLEY & THE WAILERS, 1974

This delicious reggae ramen is a tribute to the free-spirited father of the Jamaican sound and his all-time classic tune about hope. And when you're battling the despair of finishing your last mouthful, just remember his inspiring words: 'Everything's gonna be alright'.

Serves: 2–3   Preparation time: 10 minutes   Cooking time: 20 minutes

2 x 7cm piece dried kombu, rinsed
80g fresh shiitake mushrooms, sliced
4 tablespoons white miso
2cm piece of ginger, grated
4 spring onions, finely sliced

300g ramen noodles
3 small pak choi, stalks thinly sliced
60g firm tofu, cut into small cubes
1 teaspoon soy sauce

To make the dashi (or Japanese stock), place the kombu and shiitake mushrooms in a medium-sized saucepan with 1 litre of water, and bring to a simmer over a medium heat. Simmer gently for 10 minutes, being careful not to let the water boil. After 10 minutes, remove the kombu from the water. Whisk in the miso, ginger and half the spring onions.

Increase the heat to medium-high, and then add the ramen noodles to the stock. Cook for 3 minutes or until the noodles are just cooked through. Add the pak choi and tofu and continue to cook for 1 minute. Remove from the heat and stir through the soy sauce.

Serve with extra soy sauce to taste.

Hip Hop & RnB

BRAISED BEEF CHEEKS WITH CELERIAC MASH

A REMIX OF: 'RETURN OF THE MACK' BY MARK MORRISON, 1996

Despite having the voice of a chipmunk, Mark Morrison hit No. 1 in the UK and No. 2 in the USA with this catchy and rather vengeful ode to his ex-girlfriend. Now it's time for a rebound meal. If, like Mark, you've had bad luck with the chicks, move on to the cheeks.

BEEF CHEEKS:

2 tablespoons olive oil

4 beef cheeks (around 250g each)

3 onions, thinly sliced

3 garlic cloves, thinly sliced

2 fresh bay leaves

3 thyme sprigs

375ml red wine

125ml beef stock

salt and freshly ground black pepper

CELERIAC MASH:

juice of 1 lemon

1 celeriac, trimmed and peeled

1 potato, peeled and diced into 2cm pieces

250ml milk

20g butter

Preheat the oven to 150°C/gas mark 2. Heat the oil in a large flameproof casserole. Add the beef cheeks and cook over a high heat for 4–5 minutes until browned on each side, then transfer them to a plate. Reduce the heat to low, add the onion and garlic to the casserole, and sauté for 5–8 minutes or until the onion starts to turn golden. Return the cheeks and any juices to the casserole along with the bay leaves, thyme sprigs, red wine and stock. Season well with salt and pepper. Increase to a medium-high heat and bring to a simmer. Cover the pot with a lid, transfer to the oven and cook for 3½ hours or until the cheeks are tender and falling apart.

Fill a large bowl with water and the lemon juice. Chop the celeriac into 2cm pieces and place in the lemon water to prevent it from oxidising. Leave in the water and set aside until ready to use.

After the beef cheeks have been in the oven for 3 hours, put the potato and drained celeriac into a saucepan with the milk and bring to the boil over a medium-high heat. Cover and cook for 15 minutes or until the vegetables are tender. Once cooked, remove from the heat and season well with salt and pepper. Mash the celeriac, potato and milk together with a potato masher, and then stir in the butter.

Divide the celeriac mash between serving plates and top each portion with a beef cheek. Finish by spooning over the braising liquid.

NUGGETS IN PARIS

CRISPY PARMESAN & HERB CHICKEN MINI FILLETS

A REMIX OF: 'N••••S IN PARIS' BY JAY-Z AND KANYE WEST, 2011

This epic collaboration between the two kings of hip hop inspires our Grammy-worthy fusion of chicken and cheese. Replace your chef's hat with a beret and get started.

Serves: 4   Preparation time: 10 minutes   Cooking time: 30 minutes

4 slices white bread, torn into big chunks

4 tablespoons finely chopped flat-leaf parsley

40g Parmesan, grated

70g plain flour

½ teaspoon paprika

2 eggs, lightly beaten

600g chicken mini fillets

4 tablespoons olive oil, for frying

salt and freshly ground black pepper

Place the slices of bread in a food-processor and blitz into small breadcrumbs. Remove the crumbs and place in a medium-sized bowl. Add the parsley and grated Parmesan, and mix well to combine. Transfer into a shallow dish or plate.

Place the flour and paprika on a plate and season with a generous pinch of salt and pepper. Use a fork to gently mix the flour and seasonings together.

Place the beaten eggs into a shallow dish.

One at a time, dip the chicken pieces into the flour to coat, and shake off any excess. Follow by dipping gently into the beaten eggs, again shaking off any excess. Finally, roll in the breadcrumb mixture and press on the crumbs firmly to coat all sides. Repeat with the remaining pieces of chicken.

Heat half of the olive oil in a large frying pan over a medium–high heat. Cook the chicken, in batches, for 3 minutes on each side or until golden brown, crispy and cooked through. Remove from the pan onto a kitchen paper-lined plate to drain any excess oil. Cover to keep warm and repeat with the remaining chicken and oil.

Serve immediately alongside a light salad or fries.

Warning: Don't watch the dizzying collage of kaleidoscopes and strobes in the music video after eating, or you may lose your meal.

Hip Hop & RnB

I'LL BE MINCING YOU

HOMEMADE HEARTY BEEF PIES

A REMIX OF: 'I'LL BE MISSING YOU' BY PUFF DADDY AND FAITH EVANS FEAT. 112, 1997

Puff Daddy and puff pastry, a match made in heaven. This tribute to the late Notorious B.I.G. went on to become one of the biggest selling singles of all time. It mixes in a lot of The Police's 1983 hit 'Every Breath You Take'. Our tribute mixes in a lot of wine and spices.

Hip Hop & RnB

900g beef rump steak, trimmed and
chopped into small chunks

2 tablespoons olive oil

1 onion, finely chopped

2 bacon rashers, chopped into 1cm pieces

2 tablespoons tomato purée

2 tablespoons plain flour

1 tablespoon Worcestershire sauce

125ml red wine

375ml beef stock

4 sheets ready-rolled shortcrust pastry,
thawed if frozen

2 sheets puff pastry, thawed if frozen

1 egg, lightly beaten

salt and freshly ground black pepper

tomato ketchup, to serve

Put the beef pieces into a food-processor and pulse for 30 seconds or until the beef resembles mince. Set aside.

Heat a large, deep-sided frying pan over a medium-high heat. Once hot, add the oil followed by the onion and bacon. Cook and stir for 3–4 minutes or until the onion softens and the bacon starts to turn golden. Add the beef mince and continue to cook for 8–10 minutes or until brown, stirring constantly to break up any big pieces of mince. Add the tomato purée and flour and stir to combine for 2 minutes. Add the Worcestershire sauce, red wine and stock. Bring to the boil, reduce the heat to low, and simmer for 30 minutes or until the sauce thickens and resembles gravy. Season with salt and pepper to taste and then remove from the heat to cool.

Preheat the oven to 200°C/gas mark 6. Cut the shortcrust pastry sheets in half diagonally, and line eight 7.5cm pie moulds, trimming off any excess. Fill the cases with the beef mixture. Cut the puff pastry sheets into quarters and top the filled pie cases, again trimming off any excess. Use a fork to gently press the pastry edges together to seal. Use a small sharp knife to make a small cross in the pie tops. Use a pastry brush to lightly brush the tops with egg. Bake in the oven for 25–30 minutes or until golden. Leave to cool for 2 minutes and then gently remove the pies from the tin.

Serve immediately with some tomato ketchup.

• • • • • • • • • • •

'I LIKE BIG BEETS AND I CANNOT LIE'

Hip Hop & RnB

HONEY & ORANGE-GLAZED HAM

A REMIX OF: 'HOLD ON, WE'RE GOING HOME' BY DRAKE
(FEAT. MAJID JORDAN), 2013

Cause you're a good glaze and you know it... Our delicious orange-glazed ham has a lovely glistening sheen, reminiscent of the polished sounds of Canadian RnB master, Drake. And after just one bite of our tribute dish we think he'd forgive us for using honey instead of maple syrup.

Serves: 10–12   Preparation time: 20 minutes   Cooking time: 2 hours

zest and juice of 2 oranges
200g brown sugar
100ml runny honey
2 tablespoons Dijon mustard

8kg whole leg of cured, cooked ham, removed from the fridge, and set aside at room temperature for 1 hour
3 tablespoons cloves

Preheat the oven to 160°C/gas mark 3.

Put the orange zest, juice, brown sugar, honey and mustard in a medium-sized saucepan over a medium heat. Mix well to combine. Once the glaze comes to a gentle simmer, reduce the heat to medium-low, and continue to cook for 10 minutes or until the brown sugar has dissolved and the glaze begins to thicken. Remove from the heat and set aside.

Meanwhile, to prepare the ham, cut the rind from around the shank approximately 10cm from the knuckle. Remove the rind in one piece by peeling gently, leaving the fat behind. Discard the rind. Use a sharp knife to score the fat in a large diamond pattern, but do not cut right through, otherwise the meat will dry out during cooking. Stud the fat diamonds with cloves. Place the ham in a large roasting tin and spoon over half the glaze. Brush with a pastry brush to cover the ham completely, and then transfer into the oven and bake for 2 hours, basting with reserved glaze every 20 minutes.

Remove the ham from the oven, and allow to rest for 10 minutes before slicing carefully.

PASTA MOVE

BAKED POTATO GNOCCHI WITH
SLOW-ROASTED TOMATOES & BASIL

A REMIX OF: 'BUST A MOVE' BY YOUNG MC, 1989

This tasty number is inspired by a Young MC's lyrical masterpiece about a man unable to dance and impress the ladies. But have no fear, these soft spud cushions will unlock those boot shackles and get you jiving in no time. 'So come on fatso and just pasta move.'

Hip Hop & RnB

GNOCCHI:

4 x 200g floury potatoes, such as
    King Edward

40g Parmesan, finely grated, plus extra
    to serve

100g plain flour

2 egg yolks

salt and freshly ground black pepper

SAUCE:

4 tablespoons olive oil

2 garlic cloves, finely chopped

200g cherry tomatoes

2 tablespoons tomato passata

80g wild rocket, roughly chopped

Preheat the oven to 180°C/gas mark 4. Put the potatoes on a baking tray and bake for 1 hour or until soft in the centre. Set aside and allow to cool.

Once cool enough to handle, cut the potatoes in half, scoop out all of the flesh into a large bowl and discard the skins. Mash until very smooth (or pass through a potato ricer). Add the Parmesan and flour, and then season generously with salt and pepper. Add the egg yolks and stir with a wooden spoon until just combined. Place the dough onto a lightly floured surface and gently knead for 1–2 minutes until a soft dough forms. Divide the dough in two and roll each into thin lengths about 60cm long. Cut into 2cm pieces and transfer to a lightly floured tray. Cover loosely with a clean tea towel until ready to cook.

To make the sauce, place a large frying pan over a medium heat. Add the oil, followed by the garlic, and cook gently for 2 minutes, without allowing the garlic to take on too much colour. Add the cherry tomatoes and cook, stirring for a further 2–3 minutes. Add the passata and season with salt and pepper to taste. Simmer for 4–5 minutes or until the cherry tomatoes start to break down and form a sauce. If slightly dry, add a tablespoon or two of water. Remove from the heat and stir through the rocket. Set aside.

Bring a large saucepan of salted water to the boil. Cook the gnocchi in batches for 3–4 minutes or until they float to the surface and are slightly firm. Remove with a slotted spoon and place in the warm sauce.

Gently toss all the gnocchi through the sauce and serve immediately with an extra sprinkle of Parmesan.

ENCORES

KiLLiNG Me SOUFFLÉ

DOUBLE-BAKED CHEESE SOUFFLÉ

A REMIX OF: 'KILLING ME SOFTLY' BY THE FUGEES, 1996

Written in 1972 by Charles Fox and Norman Gimbel under the title 'Killing Me Softly With His Song', there have since been many great covers. But who can resist the hip-hop interpretation by the Fugees that rose to No.1 in the UK? And now your soufflé shall rise.

Hip Hop & RnB

Serves: 8   Preparation time: 15 minutes   Cooking time: 50 minutes (including cooling time)

30g unsalted butter (plus extra for greasing the ramekins)

30g plain flour

240ml full fat milk

¼ teaspoon nutmeg

3 eggs, separated

100g Cheddar, grated

100g Gruyère, grated

150ml double cream

1 tablespoon Dijon mustard

2 tablespoons chopped chives

Preheat the oven to 180°C/gas mark 4. Butter eight 90ml ramekins and set aside.

Melt the butter in a small saucepan over a medium heat. Once melted, add the flour and stir to form a smooth paste. Continue to stir for a further 30 seconds before gradually adding in the milk. Stir for a further 3–4 minutes or until the sauce thickens. Add the nutmeg and stir to combine. Set aside to cool for 5 minutes. Once the mixture has cooled slightly, beat in the egg yolks, Cheddar and half the Gruyère.

Put the egg whites in a clean bowl and whisk until soft peaks form. Mix a third of the whites into the sauce, and then gently fold through the rest of the whites with a metal spoon until just combined.

Divide the mixture evenly between the buttered ramekins, and then place them in a large roasting tin. Add hot water to the roasting tin so that it reaches halfway up the sides of the ramekins. Transfer the roasting tray carefully to the oven to cook for 20 minutes or until firm.

Remove the roasting tin and ramekins from the oven and set aside to cool. Once cool, run a sharp knife around the edges of the soufflés. Turn out the soufflés onto a baking tray lined with baking paper (or use individual roasting dishes).

Increase the oven temperature to 200°C/gas mark 6.

Mix the cream and mustard together and divide the mixture over the soufflés before scattering over the remaining Gruyère. Return the soufflés to the oven and bake for 15 minutes or until they become golden and have risen.

Sprinkle with the chopped chives and serve immediately.

Hip Hop & RnB

BAKED BRIE WITH MARINATED FIGS

A REMIX OF: 'YOUNG, WILD & FREE' BY SNOOP DOGG & WIZ KHALIFA
(FEAT. BRUNO MARS), 2011

What better way to toast the good times than with this radiant feel-good tune, some fine bubbly and our luscious starter of honeyed figs and hot, gooey brie. As Snoop might say, let's get baked.

Serves: 6–8   Preparation time: 10 minutes   Cooking time: 30 minutes

1 small wheel of brie (125–250g)

8 ripe figs, stalks trimmed

1 tablespoon balsamic vinegar

2 tablespoons extra virgin olive oil

1 tablespoon runny honey

1 orange, zested, plus 3 tablespoons juice

2 tablespoons thyme, leaves picked

3 tablespoons mint, leaves picked

crackers or slices of baguette, to serve

Preheat the oven to 180°C/gas mark 4.

Cut each fig lengthways into four wedges and place in a small, shallow dish. Set aside.

Whisk together the vinegar, oil, honey and orange juice until well combined. Pour the marinade over the figs, and scatter over the thyme and orange zest. Set aside to marinate for 20–30 minutes.

While the figs are marinating, place the unwrapped cheese in a small baking dish and bake in the preheated oven for 20 minutes or until softened. Remove the cheese from the oven and transfer to a serving platter. Allow to rest for 10 minutes.

Arrange the figs around the brie and roughly tear the mint leaves over the top.

Serve the figs and warm cheese alongside crackers or slices of baguette.

• • • • • • • • • • •

'IT'S GETTING HOT IN HERE,
SO TAKE OFF ALL YOUR CLOVES'

Hip Hop & RnB

GONNA MAKE YOU SWEET

HONEY & ROSEWATER BAKLAVA

A REMIX OF: 'GONNA MAKE YOU SWEAT (EVERYBODY DANCE NOW)'
BY C+C MUSIC FACTORY, 1990

This hip hop dance classic helped spawn the early 90s house movement and also inspired these exotic melt-in-your-mouth Turkish delights. Replace some of those lost calories from your sweat session with these perfect post-workout rewards.

Hip Hop & RnB

Makes around 30   Preparation time: 15 minutes
Cooking time: 1 hour 30 minutes (plus 6 hours cooling time)

BAKLAVA:
250g unsalted butter, melted
500g filo pastry
250g pistachios, finely chopped
250g walnuts, finely chopped
100g caster sugar
1 teaspoon ground cinnamon

SYRUP:
330g caster sugar
1 cinnamon stick
110g runny honey
5 drops rosewater
zest of 1 lemon, plus 2 tablespoons juice

Preheat the oven to 180°C/gas mark 4 and brush a 24 x 32cm baking tin with a small amount of the butter.

Cut the filo sheets to the right size to fit snugly in the tin and set aside, covered with a damp tea towel to prevent them from drying out.

Mix together the pistachios, walnuts, sugar and cinnamon in a bowl. Set aside.

Line the base of the prepared tin with a third of the filo sheets, brushing with butter between each layer. Sprinkle over half the nut mixture in an even layer, and then top with another third of the filo sheets, brushing butter between each layer. Sprinkle over the remaining nut mixture, then top with the remaining filo sheets, again brushing with butter between each layer. Refrigerate for 15 minutes or until firm.

Once the baklava is firm, use a sharp knife to score shallow criss-cross lines (4cm apart), making small diamond pieces. Bake for 50–60 minutes or until the baklava is a deep golden brown and cooked through. Use a sheet of foil to cover if it browns too quickly.

Meanwhile, to make the syrup, combine the sugar, cinnamon stick and honey with 250ml water in a medium-sized saucepan over a high heat. Stir until the sugar has completely dissolved and then bring to the boil. Once the boiling point is reached, stop stirring, reduce the heat to low and simmer for 20 minutes. Remove from the heat and strain through a fine sieve. Stir through the rosewater and lemon zest and juice, and set aside.

Once the baklava is ready, remove from the oven and cool for 5 minutes. Pour the syrup evenly over the baklava and set aside at room temperature for 6 hours or overnight.

Cut down through the score marks to loosen the diamonds and serve.

Hip Hop & RnB

WATERMELON BITES WITH PISTACHIO & ALMOND DUKKAH

A REMIX OF: 'GOLD DIGGER' BY KANYE WEST (FEAT. JAMIE FOXX), 2005

I ain't sayin' she's a gold dukkah... Forget about watching your wallet, after tasting these summer wonders your woman will only want you for your watermelon. And who can blame her. They're fruity and nutty, just like the rapper who inspired them. Sign that pre-nup and get cooking.

Makes: 20–30   Preparation time: 20 minutes   Cooking time: 5 minutes

50g sesame seeds

2 tablespoons coriander seeds

2 tablespoons cumin seeds

30g pistachios

30g almonds

½ teaspoon salt

2–2.5kg seedless watermelon

Put all the seeds, nuts and salt in a medium-sized frying pan over a medium heat. Toast for 3 minutes, stirring regularly. Remove the pan from the heat and set aside to cool completely.

Once cool, place the mixture in a food-processor (or use a pestle and mortar) and process or grind until roughly ground. Transfer to a small bowl or jar.

Cut the watermelon into large cubes, and dip the top of each cube into the dukkah before transferring to a platter.

Serve immediately.

• • • • • • • • • • •

'THINGS THAT MAKE YOU GO YUMMM...'

GOLD

DUKKAH

NUTHIN' BUTTER 'G' THANG

BUTTERMILK CRÊPES WITH RUBY RED GRAPEFRUIT & COINTREAU SAUCE

A REMIX OF: 'NUTHIN' BUT A 'G' THANG' BY DR. DRE (FEAT. SNOOP DOGG), 1992

This dope dish is derived from the first single from Dr. Dre's debut solo album. Often mistaken for 'gangsta' we believe a 'G thang' actually refers to a grapefruit, hence the recipe.

CRÊPES:

200g plain flour, sifted

4 eggs

600ml milk

400ml buttermilk

60g butter, plus extra for frying

double cream or ice cream, to serve
  (optional)

SAUCE:

2 tablespoons caster sugar

3 large ruby grapefruits, peeled, pips and
  pith removed and segmented (reserving
  any juice)

2 oranges, peeled, pips and pith removed
  and segmented (reserving any juice)

2 tablespoons Cointreau

To make the sauce, heat a large frying pan over a medium heat. Add the sugar, 1 tablespoon water and the grapefruit and orange segments, plus any juices. Stir gently and cook for a few minutes until the fruit begins to soften. Add the Cointreau and simmer for 4–5 minutes or until the sauce starts to become syrupy. Set aside.

For the crêpe batter, put the flour into a large bowl and make a well in the centre. Put the eggs, milk and buttermilk in a separate bowl or jug and gently whisk to combine. Slowly pour the wet mixture into the well in the flour while whisking. Whisk for a minute or so until there are no lumps and the batter has a consistency similar to single cream.

Melt a little butter in a crêpe pan or non-stick frying pan over a medium-high heat. Once melted, add a small ladleful of batter and swirl the pan until there is a thin, even layer of batter covering the pan. Cook for 1–2 minutes until slightly browned, and then flip and cook for a further minute. Turn out onto a plate and repeat with the rest of the batter, which should make about 12 crêpes in total. Use pieces of baking paper between the cooked crêpes to separate, and cover the plate with a clean tea towel to keep them warm.

To serve, fold a few warm crêpes into quarters on a plate, and top with a generous spoonful of the sauce.

If you wish, add a small dollop of cream or ice cream.

Hip Hop & RnB

BLUEBERRY & VANILLA
CHEESECAKE SLICE

A REMIX OF: 'ICE ICE BABY' BY VANILLA ICE, 1989

Yo, VIP, let's kick it!

This landmark tune from Vanilla Ice was the first ever hip hop single to top the Billboard charts. Not bad, considering he wrote it at the age of 16. While it's an epic track, it also has an undeniable cheese factor – hence our tribute.

Hip Hop & RnB

250g digestive biscuits, broken into large
   pieces
125g unsalted butter, melted
500g cream cheese, softened
150g caster sugar

seeds from 1 vanilla pod
zest of 1 lemon
3 eggs
125g blueberries, fresh or frozen

Preheat the oven to 150°C/gas mark 2. Line the base and sides of a 30 x 20cm baking tin with baking paper and set aside.

Put the broken biscuits in a food-processor and process for 20 seconds or until fine crumbs form. Add the melted butter and process until combined. Tip the mixture into the lined tray, and press firmly over the base and sides. Transfer the tray to the fridge for 15 minutes.

To make the filling, put the cream cheese, sugar, vanilla seeds and lemon zest in the bowl of an electric mixer. Mix on a medium speed until smooth. Add the eggs, one at a time, ensuring each one is well incorporated into the mixture before adding the next.

Remove the prepared base from the fridge and pour over the cheesecake filling, using a spatula or knife to spread it evenly. Scatter over the blueberries, and then transfer into the oven for 45–50 minutes or until just set. Remove from the oven and cool at room temperature. Transfer into the fridge for at least 2 hours until completely chilled.

Cut the cheesecake into squares and serve immediately.

'I GOT 99 PROBLEMS BUT A PEACH AIN'T ONE'

Hip Hop & RnB

PLAY THAT FUNKY MUESLI

CHOCOLATE GRANOLA WITH ROASTED STRAWBERRIES

A REMIX OF: 'PLAY THAT FUNKY MUSIC' BY WILD CHERRY, 1976

Crunchy Granola Suite has got nothing on our berry nice choccie granola. Our dish draws its inspiration from surely the most funky afro-American song ever performed by a group of white men (which was later reinterpreted by another white man, Vanilla Ice). Cereal isn't technically an instrument but you can always play the spoons. Play that funky muesli, white boy!

Serves: 8   Preparation time: 20 minutes   Cooking time: 1 hour

GRANOLA:
180g rolled oats
90g coconut flakes
125g almonds, chopped
3 tablespoons cocoa nibs
¼ teaspoon salt
125g runny honey
60ml coconut oil
30g cocoa powder
80g milk chocolate or dark chocolate chips

ROASTED STRAWBERRIES:
450g strawberries, hulled, washed and sliced
  in half
110g caster sugar
½ vanilla pod, seeds scraped
vanilla yogurt, to serve

Preheat the oven to 160°C/gas mark 3. Line a baking tray with baking paper and set aside while you prepare the granola.

Mix together the oats, coconut, almonds, cocoa nibs and salt in a large bowl.

Put the honey and coconut oil in a small saucepan over a medium-low heat and stir together until the mixture begins to simmer. Whisk in the cocoa, and then pour the mixture over the dry ingredients, and stir well to coat evenly.

CONTINUED OVERLEAF

Hip Hop & RnB

Tip the mixture into the prepared tray and spread out in an even layer. Bake for 35 minutes, stirring every 10 minutes until the granola is toasted. Remove from the oven and allow to cool for 20–30 minutes. Once the granola is almost completely cool, break it into clusters and drop into a large bowl, and then stir through the chocolate chips. The granola will keep in an airtight container for up to 1 month.

To make the roasted strawberries, preheat the oven to 200°C/gas mark 6. Place the strawberries, sugar and vanilla seeds in a large bowl and toss well to coat. Transfer the strawberries to a baking dish and arrange in an even layer. Place the baking dish in the preheated oven to roast for 15 minutes, stirring halfway through the cooking time. Remove the strawberries from the oven and cool completely.

Serve with the chocolate granola and a spoonful of vanilla yogurt.

• • • • • • • • • • •

'NIBBLE IT, JUST A LITTLE BIT'

Hip Hop & RnB

EVERYDAY PAWPAW

CREAMY COCONUT RICE WITH BLUEBERRIES & PAWPAW

A REMIX OF: 'PEOPLE EVERYDAY' BY ARRESTED DEVELOPMENT, 1992

'Everyday People' by Sly and The Family Stone reached the top spot in the USA in 1968, but it's the later interpretation by hip hop group Arrested Development that we find especially tasty. The song calls for equality between races and social groups, while our dish achieves tastebud harmony between papaya (pawpaw) and blueberries.

Serves: 4   Preparation time: 10 minutes   Cooking time: 2 hours (including cooling time)

20g butter, softened
80g short grain rice
65g caster sugar
400ml coconut milk
1 vanilla pod, halved lengthways

¼ papaya, halved, deseeded, peeled and cubed
40g blueberries
zest and juice of 1 lime
50ml double cream

Preheat the oven to 150°C/gas mark 2. Grease a 1.5-litre ovenproof dish with the softened butter. Combine the rice, sugar, coconut milk and 400ml water in a large bowl or jug. Pour into the prepared dish and add the vanilla pod. Bake for 1 hour and 45 minutes until the rice is tender, stirring every 20 minutes. Remove from the oven and leave to cool completely, then remove the vanilla pod and refrigerate for 1 hour.

Meanwhile, combine the papaya, blueberries and lime zest and juice in a small bowl. When ready to serve, lightly whip the cream until soft peaks form. Gently fold the cream through the rice mixture and serve in bowls topped with a spoonful of the fruit.

INDEX

190   Index

I hope you had the Thai of your life

MANY SHANKS

Kyle Books have enabled me to fulfill a lifelong dream of infusing seriously good food with not-so-subtle hints of stupidity.

Respect to Kyle Cathie for her belief and to Tara O'Sullivan for her tireless work, positivity and extra large portion of patience. With designer Louise Leffler and Nic Jones and Gemma John in production, you guys make a cracking quintet.

A massive bow to the supremely talented Karina Duncan, the culinary conductor of *Killing Me Soufflé*. This gig wouldn't have gone off without her creativity, huge effort and stovetop prowess.

I'm in awe of Marylou Faure's outrageous flair with a pencil and super thankful for her ability to stir in the visual nuttiness.

Praise too for Jay Hynes, Jesse Marlow and legal eagle Michael Tucak for all their support.

And finally a 'hip hop hooray' to Leah Dunkley for inspiring all this silliness, with what began as a bowl of soup named David Lee Broth in 2010. Thanks for all the sage tips and pep talks whenever I was throwing in the spatula. You're a good egg.